I SURRENDER ALL

I SURRENDER ALL

REBUILDING A MARRIAGE BROKEN BY PORNOGRAPHY

CLAY AND RENEE CROSSE
with Mark Tabb

NAVPRESS®

BRINGING TRUTH TO LIFE

OUR GUARANTEE TO YOU

We believe so strongly in the message of our books that we are making this quality guarantee to you. If for any reason you are disappointed with the content of this book, return the title page to us with your name and address and we will refund to you the list price of the book. To help us serve you better, please briefly describe why you were disappointed. Mail your refund request to: NavPress, P.O. Box 35002, Colorado Springs, CO 80935.

The Navigators is an international Christian organization. Our mission is to reach, disciple, and equip people to know Christ and to make Him known through successive generations. We envision multitudes of diverse people in the United States and every other nation who have a passionate love for Christ, live a lifestyle of sharing Christ's love, and multiply spiritual laborers among those without Christ.

NavPress is the publishing ministry of The Navigators. NavPress publications help believers learn biblical truth and apply what they learn to their lives and ministries. Our mission is to stimulate spiritual formation among our readers.

ISBN 1-57683-732-7

Cover design by Disciple Design
Cover illustration Kristin Barlow
Creative Team: Terry Behimer, Liz Heaney, Arvid Wallen, Kathy Mosier, Glynese Northam

Some of the anecdotal illustrations in this book are true to life and are included with the permission of the persons involved. All other illustrations are composites of real situations, and any resemblance to people living or dead is coincidental.

Unless otherwise identified, all Scripture quotations in this publication are taken from the Holy Bible, New Living Translation (NLT), copyright © 1996. Used by permission of Tyndale House Publishers, Inc., Wheaton, Illinois 60189. All rights reserved. Other versions used include: the HOLY BIBLE: NEW INTERNATIONAL VERSION˚ (NIV˚), Copyright © 1973, 1978, 1984 by International Bible Society, used by permission of Zondervan Publishing House, all rights reserved; THE MESSAGE (MSG). Copyright © 1993, 1994, 1995, 1996, 2000, 2001, 2002. Used by permission of NavPress Publishing Group; and the New King James Version (NKJV). Copyright © 1982 by Thomas Nelson, Inc. Used by permission. All rights reserved.

Crosse, Clay.
  I surrender all : rebuilding a marriage broken by pornography / Clay
and Renee Crosse, with Mark Tabb.
    p. cm.
  ISBN 1-57683-732-7
  1. Sex--Religious aspects--Christianity. 2. Sex in marriage. 3.
Marriage--Religious aspects--Christianity. 4. Crosse, Clay. I. Crosse,
Renee, 1970- II. Tabb, Mark A. III. Title.
  BT708.C75 2005
  228.8'44--dc22
                        2005006776
Printed in ***CHECK COUNTRY***

1 2 3 4 5 6 7 8 9 10 / 09 08 07 06 05

FOR A FREE CATALOG OF
NAVPRESS BOOKS & BIBLE STUDIES,
CALL 1-800-366-7788 (USA)
OR 1-800-839-4769 (CANADA)

CONTENTS

PREFACE

I stand here on the other side, looking back at a war that almost destroyed me. That war was fueled by pornography. Porn is a killer, and it won't stop until something is dead. I know many men look at it and don't see the danger. "It's just a little harmless fantasy," they reason. Meanwhile, their minds are being poisoned. Their lives are changing for the worse. They are becoming calloused to what's really important in their lives: first and foremost, their relationship with God; their marriage; their children; their church; their career. All of these feel the negative effects of a man viewing pornography. In one way or another, they all suffer. If he continues on that path, destruction will follow.

Renee and I want to reach out to families who are either going through this problem or might be casually slipping to a similar place of harm. It can be such a subtle slide. We know this firsthand because it was a casual and subtle slide that drove me to the depths that we describe in this book. Thankfully, we end by telling an account of God's grace and healing in our lives and the plan He had for us all along. He has lovingly brought us through the story you are about to read. It has been awesome to feel His hand on us throughout the whole journey.

We have been blessed to be able to share our testimony in this book in addition to speaking at marriage enrichment conferences and various events nationwide. Audiences everywhere listen to this story with great interest. After we've finished speaking, it never fails that people come up to us and want to talk about their lives. It's amazing, and it's very telling. They say things such as, "You know, you were up there telling our story. My husband and I recently went through the very same thing!" Others tell us of failed marriages in their past. Some tell us that their spouse is struggling, and they don't know how they will recover as a couple. This has happened time and time again everywhere we've gone. After hearing it enough times, we began to realize that our story is one that is being lived out in homes everywhere. We are not alone in this. Far from it.

The challenge is this: Christian homes should function in a different way than non-Christian homes, don't you think? A better way. A more loving and caring way. A less destructive and hurtful way. Doesn't it only make sense that a home dedicated to serving and glorifying God would look different than a home that doesn't acknowledge God? It should be very simple.

And yet the sad reality is that there are many, many Christian (churchgoing) families who are in no better shape than families who don't serve God or attend church. The same issues seem to surface from home to home. The same hurts. The same needs. The same temptations. The same failures. They unhappily struggle along, and a staggering percentage of them just give up and throw in the towel.

Renee and I feel a strong calling to challenge and warn other couples. *Warn* might seem like a dramatic word, but it is precisely what is needed. A blaring alarm. A loud siren. A deadly-storm warning. To not warn couples out there would put Renee and me in a place that the prophet Isaiah spoke of: "For the leaders of my people — the LORD's watchmen, his shepherds — are blind to every danger. They are like silent watchdogs that give no warning when danger comes" (Isaiah 56:10).

It's no secret that our homes are under serious attack. Our homes and marriages will fall without intentional safeguards in place. We have found that the casual, "whatever" lifestyle will destroy us. We should care more about our homes than that. We should take the responsibility of husband, wife, mommy, or daddy much more seriously than we sometimes do.

God wants the best for you, and so do we. We really do! Renee and I have felt such an incredible change since our recommitment to each other and to God in 1998, and we want to see other marriages thrive and truly begin to grow. While marriage can be incredibly great, we also know that there is a fine line between, "Everything's wonderful!" and "We are sinking." We have known couples who at one point looked indestructible — the perfect family. Then, one day, everything imploded.

We pray this book will be a message of both warning *and* hope for you. Warning of the arrows that are likely aimed at your home right now and the hope of an amazing and protected life fully dedicated to God.

Clay Crosse

ACKNOWLEDGMENTS

The process of writing this book has been a joy and an education for us. We want to say a big "Thanks!" to the following folks:

Mark Tabb. You have been a joy to know and work with. You are a man of God, and we are blessed to have partnered with you on this project.

Terry Behimer and all the fine people at NavPress. Your excitement from day one has meant so much to us. May God bless this effort.

Jason Catron and *Neutron Entertainment.* You are a dear friend and teammate. May Holy Homes spring up worldwide!

Pastor Dana Key and *The Love of Christ Church* in Memphis, Tennessee. You keep us plugged in and planted. We love you so much!

David Breen and *The Breen Agency.*

Lifeway Festival of Marriage events.

Moody Bible Institute marriage events.

Extraordinary Women conferences.

And to all our *friends and family* who have been there for us. Thank you for the love, support, and prayers.

COASTING
TOWARD
SODOM

Clay

NO PLACE TO HIDE

I was running out of options. Nothing had worked. The doctors kept telling me nothing was physically wrong. Most people would consider that good news, but I didn't. I'd been poked and prodded and had a scope stuck down my throat, all to no avail. The voice specialists and otolaryngologists at the Vanderbilt Voice Center told me my vocal chords looked healthy and everything appeared to be normal. "Then why can't I sing?" I asked. They didn't know. I expected them to tell me I'd overstressed a vocal chord or that a polyp had developed that had to be removed. I wanted the doctors to say that I needed surgery and that after six months of rest and rehabilitation, my voice would be as good as new. Instead they gave me a clean bill of health but no answers. I was running out of options.

I was also running out of time. Weeks were quickly turning into months, and I wasn't getting any better. The problem with my voice had shown up a few months earlier when I came down with a sinus infection during a tour stop in Savannah. At the time I didn't think much of it. I usually get at least one sinus infection a year. The show had to go on, so I sang through the infection as best I could. That wasn't saying much. I couldn't hit the notes my songs demanded. On the rare occasions I did, I couldn't hold them. Still, everyone was supportive. They knew I was sick. I thought I could attack the illness with antibiotics and rest and be back to normal in no time.

ATTENTION GETTER

The sinus infection went away, but my voice still didn't return. As days turned into weeks, I started to wonder if it ever would. Night after night I went out on stage, but every song was a battle. Singing had always been almost effortless for me, but now my voice wobbled and broke. Crowds still came, but their response had changed. The standing ovations had ended, and the compliments had stopped. My managers and Renee, my wife, kept telling me to hang in there, that it was just a matter of time before everything returned to normal. But as the months dragged by, I began to doubt if I would ever again have the voice I once took for granted.

My fears came crashing down on me later that summer when World Vision invited me to their headquarters in Seattle to sing for a staff chapel service. The day was a disaster. To make matters worse, my friends from the group Avalon were in the audience. As an artist, I always feel pressure to do my absolute best in front of my peers. But that day my best stunk. I felt embarrassed and began to wonder what I would do if I couldn't sing anymore. That night back at the hotel, I tossed and turned, unable to sleep. Over and over I prayed, *God, what is happening to me?*

The next day I flew from Seattle back to Nashville. As the plane headed east, the sky grew dark and so did my thoughts. I tried to imagine my life without music, but the picture sent a chill down my spine. Singing had been my life for so long that I couldn't imagine doing anything else. Nor did I want to. I had to sing, not just because of the drive inside me, but because my voice was my family's only source of income. If my career suddenly ended, I had no idea what I would do to pay the bills and keep food on our table.

My mood grew even darker as I began to think about Renee and our two daughters, Shelby and Savannah. How was I going to take care of them? Maybe they'd be better off without me. After all, my life insurance policy would set them up for life. That's when I started praying, *Come on, Lord. Get me out of here. Just take me home.* I knew Renee would mourn for a while, but I also knew she would eventually meet someone else, someone whose life wasn't so messed up.

Reading this, you might think I overreacted to my voice problems. Why would I want to die just because I couldn't sing the way I always had? Sitting alone on that long plane ride, I started to think clearly for the first time in a long time. No one knew it, not even my wife, but I'd been living a lie. I'd made a career out of singing songs about God, but I didn't live what I sang. Far from it. I lived for Clay. And more and more over the past two years, I'd lived for the rush I found in watching pornographic videos and the quick sexual release that followed. At first all this was just a game to me, just another way of entertaining myself. But finally I realized the cycle of porn, lust, and sexual fantasies had me in their grip. My personal life was spinning out of control, and I knew that given the opportunity, I would do something that would destroy my marriage.

No wonder the doctors can't find anything wrong with me, I thought to myself. *It's not my voice. It's me.* For the first time, I connected the dots God had shoved in my face. I looked out the window, tears streaming down my face, and prayed, *Lord, is it this simple? Did you take away my singing voice because of my wicked desires? Are you trying to get my attention?* As I made this connection, I started to get angry with God. *No way! That can't be what's happening. My voice will come back . . . won't it?* Suddenly I saw where my life was heading. No Renee. No family. No career. No respect. No dignity. Nothing. *Oh, God, please let this plane crash and just end it all!*

17

CAUGHT

Obviously, God didn't answer my prayer. My plane didn't crash, and I made it home safely. Walking through the door helped me regain a bit of my sanity, and I convinced myself I'd been a little too hard on myself on the plane. I told myself I wasn't perfect and there were things in my life that probably shouldn't be there, but that only made me like everyone else. My real problem remained what it had been before I got on the plane: my voice. I had to find an answer for my voice. And soon.

My search for an answer led me to call Chris Beatty, a highly respected voice coach in Nashville who has worked with everyone from Keith Green to Dan Haseltine of Jars of Clay. If there was nothing wrong with me physically, then something had to be wrong with my vocal technique. I hoped Chris would be able to point out some defect in the way I was singing. Maybe then I could recover what I'd lost and get my voice back.

I walked into his studio and flopped down in a chair across from his keyboard. Chris sat on the opposite side. "So, what's going on with your voice?" he asked.

His question opened the floodgates. I told him my life story in a nutshell, starting with growing up in Memphis and my dreams of becoming a singer. From there I told him about sending out demo tapes and praying for the big break that finally came. Everything centered on my voice: how it once worked, the range I had, and the day it let me down in Savannah. While I talked, Chris just leaned back in his chair and listened. Occasionally he would nod as if to say, "Yes, I've heard this before. I can fix this." His eyes never left mine as he sat and rubbed his chin, taking it all in. When I finally finished, I let out a long sigh and sank down in my chair. "So," I asked, "can you help me?"

Chris is a tall, fatherly figure with thinning gray hair and eyes that seem to look right through you. He didn't say anything for what felt like forever. I shifted in my seat, uncomfortable with his silence. Finally Chris leaned across his keyboard, looked me in the eye, and asked, "Clay, are you a man of God?"

What? I thought. This wasn't what I had expected to hear. I thought this expert voice coach would tell me I wasn't holding my head right or that my breathing techniques were wrong. I came to him to fix my vocal mechanics, not dive into my personal life. But I didn't say what I was thinking. I didn't say anything.

Chris paused before hitting me with another question. "Do you have a daily prayer life, and do you spend time each day in the Word?" he asked. He paused again while I sat in silence, looking up at him. Finally he asked, "Clay, how's your marriage? What's your relationship like with your wife?" Then he leaned back in his chair and waited for me to answer.

But I couldn't. I couldn't say a word. A man I'd known all of ten minutes was asking for intimate details of my personal life. I am not sure why I didn't jump up and tell him, "What right do you have to ask me that? Tell me what's wrong with my voice!" But I didn't. I was caught. I had no place to hide.

Chris's eyes never left me. He didn't say another word; he didn't need to. The Holy Spirit had already said enough through him. Later Chris told me God had prompted him to ask me those three questions. He knew nothing of my secret. But in that moment I thought he did. I felt as though Chris could see right through my lies to the real me. Rather than dealing with my sin head-on, I had swept it under the rug and hoped it would take care of itself. It hadn't.

Sitting before Chris, I knew I couldn't hide from my sin any longer. Another lie tried to rush through my mind, telling me that because

I would sometimes go weeks without watching porn, I couldn't be addicted to it. I looked over at Chris and knew I couldn't keep lying to myself. I dropped my head in shame. Tears began to well up. I opened my mouth to speak but couldn't. As all the games I'd played with God and all the lies I'd told myself to justify my sin crumbled to the ground, my tears grew into uncontrollable sobs, and I shook all over.

Chris walked over to me, placed his hand on my shoulder, and began to pray. It was as though God Himself had entered the room and was speaking directly to my soul. After Chris prayed, I prayed. My words were nothing like my pitiful prayer on the plane. I came clean with God. I had known I had sin in my life, but I had chosen not to notice the incredible distance I'd kept between God and me. I felt incredible shame for the images in my head and the thoughts I entertained day in and day out. But more than that, I felt ashamed of the grief I'd caused God. I pleaded with Him to forgive me. Chris's simple questions made me realize that the direction of my life was wrong and had been for a very long time.

After the tears stopped, Chris gave me some basics on how to rebuild my relationship with the Lord. He told me to spend time in prayer each day using the Lord's Prayer as a model. He also told me to read a chapter of Proverbs every morning. Above all, he stressed to me how my career meant far less than my relationships with God and with my wife and daughters. If they weren't right, my music was nothing but noise.

As I left Chris's office, I knew this was only the beginning. Though I was finally moving toward God instead of running away from Him, one afternoon of confession and prayer didn't suddenly make me immune to temptation any more than it made me a man of God. That would take time. Lots of time. I still had a long way to go to get where I needed to be. I needed to set some things right; I needed to talk to my wife.

I knew telling Renee my secrets would hurt both of us. I didn't know how she'd respond, but I also knew I didn't have a choice. I had to confess my sins to her if I was going to be a different person than I was before. Renee didn't know it, but I'd driven us to the brink of divorce. If God had not intervened, I would have had an affair, and in the eyes of God I already had because Jesus said looking lustfully at another woman is the same as sleeping with her. How do you tell the woman you promised to love, honor, and cherish something like that? But I had to. I had to come clean. I'd kept too many secrets for far too long. Driving home, I began to prepare myself for the hardest talk we would ever have.

2

CRACKS IN THE FOUNDATION

I didn't talk to Renee about my conversation with Chris the minute I walked in the door. She asked how everything went and I told her "fine," but I didn't go into much detail. Not yet. I needed more time to figure out what I would say. How could I tell my wife, the woman I'd claimed was the love of my life since we started dating fourteen years earlier, that I'd watched pornographic videos on a regular basis and fantasized about other women on a daily basis for the past two years? I couldn't just walk in the door and say, "Hi, honey, I'm home. Oh, by the way, I watch porn and dream about having sex with any nameless and faceless woman that might jump in my bed. But don't worry, Chris helped me get right with God and I'm all better now. What's for dinner?" Yeah, like that would work. I knew Renee would be angry and there would be lots and lots of tears, but I thought she would be willing to forgive me. At least I hoped she would.

I spent the next few days trying to figure out what I would say to her. The joy and release I felt at Chris's office gave way to dread. I prayed like I never had before. One question kept running through my head: *How did I get myself in this mess?* The answer might surprise you. It surprised me.

As I contemplated the mess I'd made of my life, I realized my problem went beyond watching pornographic movies and entertaining sexual fantasies of other women. Even if I had never watched anything more graphic than *Winnie-the-Pooh*, my life still would not have been right. I had been on a slippery slope for years. Although I'd asked Jesus to save me from my sins when I was thirteen, I'd never obeyed the simplest and most basic commandment of all. Instead of loving the Lord my God with all my heart and mind and strength and soul, I had regarded Him as little more than fire insurance that would keep me out of hell. I entrusted Him with my eternal soul, but my life showed no signs of any passion for Him. I was a casual Christian coasting along in the world. I had a ticket to heaven in my pocket that I thought gave me a free ride to live any way I wanted.

Even more than my problem with lust, my greatest affront to God was my failure to follow Him in even the most basic areas of life. Sometimes I think I would have been better off if I had simply been an out-and-out pagan. I probably would have been more honest if I had spent my high school years drinking and carousing and doing everything I could to avoid God. At least then I would have been spiritually ice-cold. Instead, I spent the first eighteen years of my Christian life lukewarm.

I know some of you reading this will think I have it backward. After all, contemplating an affair with any woman who would make herself available to me is a horrible sin. Not reading my Bible or praying might seem pretty tame in comparison. But it isn't. God made it pretty clear how He feels about lukewarm Christians. He told the church in Laodicea, "I know your works, that you are neither cold nor hot. I could wish you were cold or hot. So then, because you are lukewarm, and neither cold nor hot, I will vomit you out of My mouth" (Revelation 3:15-16, NKJV). My lukewarm spiritual life made God sick. Looking back, it does me as well.

BACK TO THE BEGINNING

I never set out to become spiritually nauseating. While I was growing up, that was the last thing I thought I would be. For as far back as I can remember, my parents took me to church. All my life I knew about God and Jesus and the gospel. Being exposed to Christianity didn't make me a Christian, though. I had to come to a point where I felt a need for Him myself. That happened on a trip with our church's youth choir when I was thirteen.

Our choir director was John Ellzey, a man with a passion for telling people about Jesus. He taught us a lot about music, but he cared far more about reaching people for Christ. Music always played a secondary role to the message. During the school year, Mr. Ellzey would work with us on some sort of musical presentation. Then, during the summer, he would take us on the road. Even though we never left the country, we called those excursions mission trips. We would travel to some other state and plug into local churches, putting on revivals at night and going door-to-door during the day, witnessing and inviting people to the revivals.

Mr. Ellzey amazed me. I'd never seen anyone who cared so deeply about the eternal destiny of people he didn't even know. In 1980, during a mission trip, I felt drawn to Christ in a way I never had before. I prayed and asked Jesus to forgive me and to come into my life and become my Lord and Savior. And He did. I've never doubted that Jesus Christ came into my life that summer. From that point forward, God and church played a major role in my life. Throughout junior high and high school, our church youth group was the focal point of my social life. I stuck with Mr. Ellzey and kept singing in his choir.

Not only was I involved in the youth choir, but I also played in all the church sports leagues and attended youth group every Sunday and

Wednesday night. All of my friends were there. We'd go to Wendy's or Pizza Hut after church and then top off the evening with a round of miniature golf at Putt-Putt. Church was the one place where I completely belonged. I didn't feel the pressure to conform to the crowd that I felt at school. Being a Christian is hard enough. Trying to be a Christian in a typical high school can be nearly impossible. The other kids make you feel like a complete loser if you don't drink or cuss or brag about your sexual exploits from the past weekend. At least that's how it was for me in school. I was never part of the popular crowd, so church was my oasis. I had a close-knit group of friends there. We hung out together, which made it easier for all of us to be consistent in our claims of following Christ.

MILE-WIDE, INCH-DEEP

Even though I went to church almost every time the doors were open and other believers were my closest friends, it doesn't mean I had a good relationship with Christ. In fact, I didn't have much of a relationship at all. I didn't talk with God in prayer, and I didn't listen to what He had to tell me in His Word. I never read my Bible except for a random verse or two during Sunday school. Oh, I carried it with me to youth group, and I knew where to find most of the books, but I never read it, not the way you should if you want to get to know God intimately. And I rarely prayed except when something really bad happened. Everyone prays during a crisis, and I was no different. Those prayers were heartfelt and real, but prayer wasn't a regular part of my life. I didn't have anything even close to a daily walk with Jesus. Instead, I kept God on retainer. Months could go by when I didn't need Him, but the moment something bad happened, I would make the call. To say my spiritual life was shallow is an understatement.

Although my walk with God was shallow, I still had some strong convictions. I drew a line in the sand on certain issues, especially drinking. Kids at school constantly talked about getting wasted. The whole idea sounded so foreign to me. I knew that being a Christian meant I had to be different. Several of my church friends and I made commitments to never drink alcohol. We didn't make a big deal about it at school, but people knew. To this day I still haven't had a drink, not that this makes God applaud. I can't say I took this stand out of love for Christ. In my mind, alcohol formed the line separating believers and nonbelievers. Not drinking was simply part of my identity as a Christian.

I wore the label of "Christian," but I failed to go deeper with Christ. Sure, I went to church all the time, but I went because that's where my friends were. I went for the softball leagues and the choir and the social life. Youth group, pizza, and miniature golf — all with a group of good Christian kids. I never really thought there needed to be something more. Something deeper. Something beyond casual Christianity. After all, I knew I would go to heaven when I died. What more did I need?

DANGEROUS COMPROMISE

My superficial understanding of the Christian life opened the door for dangerous compromise. James 3:2 says, "We all stumble in many ways" (NIV). This simply means we all have areas of weakness in which we are most vulnerable to temptation. Pornography and the lust it unleashes are mine.

My first exposure to porn came in the fourth grade. I was at a friend's house after school when his parents weren't home, and we found his dad's fairly extensive collection of magazines. I'd never seen anything like those pictures, and they fascinated me. A few years later, another friend brought out a movie. Again, his parents weren't home. Deep down I knew looking at this material was wrong, but I never knew how dangerous it was. After all, my friends' dads had it. How bad could it be?

It wasn't like my buddies and I made a habit of viewing pornography. Back then, I would catch an occasional glimpse; that was all. I didn't seek it out. I didn't buy any of my own. But if the opportunity to look at pictures of naked women presented itself, I took it. No one ever told me those images would burn themselves into my mind and come back to haunt me. I wish someone had.

By the time I was in high school, I had a few magazines hidden in my room. I should have seen this as a warning signal of a growing problem, but I disregarded any such thoughts. Even after Renee and I started dating and made public commitments to sexual purity, I still didn't see the danger of pornography. I always equated purity with not having sex, and since I'd not had sex, I thought I was doing okay. But deep down I felt as if I must be the only twenty-year-old virgin in the entire world, and I resented it.

To be honest, Renee's commitment to purity was much stronger than mine. That's an understatement. I would have given in had she just said the word. More than once she told me that just because I was three years older than she was, I shouldn't think I could talk her into doing something she wasn't going to do. When I returned home from my freshman year of college, I told Renee I was tired of waiting until we got married before we had sex. "If you love me, you will do this," I told her. I'm not proud of this, but I don't want to give the impression that I was something I wasn't. She told me that if I kept pressuring her to have sex, our relationship would be over. Even though she loved me, her commitment to purity meant more to her than holding on to a jerk of a boyfriend who was trying to talk her into things she didn't want to do. I backed off and accepted the fact that Renee was serious about remaining sexually pure. I knew if I truly loved her, I needed to get serious as well. I stopped pushing, which helped our relationship immensely.

I was so out of touch with God that I was able to convince myself that He was okay with my using pornography because it provided me with a "safe" release for my lust. But pornography works as a catalyst on the body. Pictures of naked women or images of people having sex on a screen ignite a fire inside that has to be satisfied. They kick the natural sex drive into hyperdrive. The sex drive itself isn't a bad thing. God designed this drive to work inside a marriage to draw a husband and wife closer to one another in love as they become one flesh. But porn revs up this drive and excites lust, not love. God's gift of sex within marriage leads both partners to give themselves to one another. But lust does just the opposite. It moves the focus entirely upon one's self, so rather than wanting to give of yourself, you want to take. You want satisfaction. And because the other party in this false romance is nothing more than an image on a screen or in a magazine, the desire for satisfaction leads to masturbation. My body became conditioned to this cycle, and I began to think about sex so much that I could hardly think about anything else. I liked the feeling lust built up inside me, and I could get it quickly with porn. All the while I told myself, *Well, at least Renee and I aren't sleeping together.*

But the damage from pornography doesn't end when the video stops or the magazine is thrown away. If I was in a store and saw a good-looking woman, I could transpose what I'd seen on to her. She stopped being a human being and became nothing more than a sex object. It's sad to think I could have been so blind. I wish someone had told me what I'm telling you.

Pornography, like most sin, operates under the principle of

diminishing returns. Over time, the magazines that once gave me a thrill and a sexual release didn't give me the same buzz, so I had to find something more graphic in order to get the same effect. My use of porn progressed beyond magazines when one of my friends and I started going to an adult theater. This should have been a big red flag, but I didn't see it as such. I didn't understand how the law of diminishing returns was driving me to sink deeper into this habit. Sin always works like this. It keeps pushing and building until it messes up your entire life. By seeking sexual release through pornography and masturbation, I was conditioning my mind and body to react in the wrong way. The mind is like a savings account. The more we deposit into it, the greater the account, along with the interest, grows. I was depositing pornographic images into my mind and had built up a level of lust and desire that caused me to think about sex constantly. Yet at the same time, I thought I was keeping a commitment to sexual purity because my future wife and I weren't sleeping together. I can't believe anyone could be so stupid as to play this insane game.

The two parts of this story sound as though they couldn't possibly go together. How could I have claimed to be a Christian and yet have allowed pornography into my life? Unfortunately, at the time I didn't see the contradiction. I thought of porn as a form of entertainment instead of sin, and I saw my use of pornography as only temporary. Renee was the one I really wanted, not some body in a magazine. As soon as Renee and I were married, I would walk away from pornography and never go back. My plan worked — for a while.

GOD'S GRACE IS ALWAYS PRESENT

As I look back, I realize that my conscience would never have been so dull if I had pursued the kind of relationship God wanted to have with me. I settled for something so shallow, so ho-hum, when I could have had much more.

Still, God's love and grace toward me never changed. My secret life grieved Him, but He never stopped loving me. He never stopped treating me like His child. Even during this period of my life when God was far from my daily thoughts, evidence of His grace surrounded me. I learned firsthand the truth of 2 Timothy 2:13:

> If we are unfaithful,
> > he remains faithful,
> > for he cannot deny himself.

He brought Renee and me together, and He enabled us to wear white on our wedding day. He called out to me and pulled me toward Himself in spite of me. Like any good parent, He refused to abandon me to the poor choices I had made.

3

MORE THAN I ASKED FOR

When Renee and I finally got married, I felt relieved that my battles with pornography and lust would be finished. I thought that because my days of waiting to have sex were over, all my problems would be solved. I convinced myself that any old habits were now completely behind me. After all, I wouldn't need pornography for sexual release any longer. So why would I want it? I had a beautiful wife who loved me. What more could any man ask for? I threw out any traces of pornography and vowed to walk away from it, never to return.

Our wedding day felt like a fresh start for me. As I stood at the front of our home church wearing a white tux and waiting for my bride to walk down the aisle, I thanked God that we had remained virgins. Renee wanted us both to wear white as a testimony to our church. We saw this as a way of glorifying God in our wedding ceremony and telling other young couples that it is possible to wait for sex until marriage. As I watched my bride coming down the aisle toward me, I realized God had given me a great blessing in her. In that moment I knew more than ever before that I wanted our lives to be different. I wanted us to stand out from the world and shine for God. Unfortunately, eight years would pass before I would begin to do the work to make this desire a reality.

DREAMING OF POSSIBILITIES

Our first house was what Renee called cozy. Small comes closer to the truth. Very small. Her mother jokingly called it a cracker box the first time she saw it. We didn't care. It had room enough for the two of us, and that was all that mattered. Our schedules kept us from spending as much time together as we wanted. Renee worked at a mortgage company during the day, and I worked nights at FedEx. I hoped to get promoted to a delivery job so that we could have the same work schedules, but those positions were hard to come by in Memphis. I was also attending classes at Memphis State during the day.

Later that year I joined a jazz vocal ensemble at Memphis State called Sound Fuzion. The Memphis Symphony Orchestra invited us to sing with them for one performance. I'd been singing in front of audiences for five years, but this was different. I'll never forget the adrenaline rush of singing with a full orchestra behind me. This was nothing like the garage bands I'd played in throughout high school. As part of the concert, I stood center stage and sang the Simon and Garfunkel classic "Bridge over Troubled Water." I've always loved that song, but with the orchestra welling up behind me, I felt the music like I never had before. By the time I reached the last note, I knew I wouldn't spend the next thirty-five years shuffling packages. I could spiritualize the moment and say that was when God called me into music as a vocation, but I wasn't thinking in those terms at that time. All I knew was from that day forward music would be my life. I had to be a singer.

NASHVILLE OR BUST

Of course, saying I was going to make it in the music business and actually doing it were worlds apart. Since high school, I'd been singing every chance I got, and during my summer breaks from college, I had a job singing with one of the musicals at a local theme park, Libertyland. Even after I started working at FedEx, I sang anywhere and everywhere I could. Churches. Weddings. Funerals. It didn't matter. If someone asked me to sing, I was there. I had always hoped music could become more than a hobby, but up until that point, I hadn't had a burning desire to make it happen.

Everything changed the night I sang with the Memphis Symphony Orchestra. But I had one small problem: I had no idea what I needed to do to make my dream a reality. People would pat me on the back and tell me to go for it, but no one could tell me how. *American Idol* didn't hit the airwaves for another dozen years. I did win a local talent show and a trip to Hollywood with an audition at the CBS television studios, but nothing came of it. Part of me wondered if anything with my music ever would.

Finally Steve Wickliffe, a close friend of mine, offered to finance a demo tape for me. I covered some of my favorite Christian songs, and we started sending the tape to anyone and everyone in the industry we could get in touch with. Initially the tape produced nothing but a string of letters that were all variations of "Thank you for your interest. However, we regret to inform you that the tape is not what we are looking for at the present time." A few said they didn't have time to get involved with anyone new. Every day it looked more and more as if my music would never go anywhere, yet I never doubted my voice or my ability to make it. I kept asking God, "Why would You give me this voice if You didn't want me to use it full-time?" This prayer rolled off my lips day and night as I thought about nothing but singing. My dream was quickly becoming an obsession. Renee supported me every step of the way, as this was her dream as well. Yet neither of us thought much about how my voice could be used for God's glory. To me, music meant entertainment, not ministry.

Even after my career took off and awards started rolling in, I continued to see myself as an entertainer, not a minister. I hadn't progressed very far from the shallow spirituality I had as a teenager. My sole desire was to make it as a musician, which to me meant making a comfortable living through music. I looked at the biggest stars in both the Christian and secular markets and told myself that would be me someday. Again, I prayed and asked God to open doors, but my focus remained on me and what I thought was best for my career.

SEEDS OF SUCCESS

Not long after I started sending out demo tapes, I saw an ad in the paper announcing a Gary McSpadden concert at a nearby church. Gary had been part of the Bill Gaither Trio and the Gaither Vocal Band before launching a solo career. As I read the ad, the wheels in my head started spinning. *I've got to get a copy of my tape into his hands*, I told myself. I didn't know Gary, but I knew he was inside the industry. I needed a break, and I thought he might open some doors for me. I didn't ask myself why he would listen to the tape or help us. By this point I was desperate, and desperate people will try anything.

After the concert, Renee and I waited around until the auditorium was almost empty before approaching Gary. We walked up and introduced ourselves. I started telling him about my voice and my dream. I know how exhausted Gary had to have been, but he never showed it. Instead he listened to me go on and on. When I offered him my demo tape, he took it and promised to listen to it. Just then his manager, Ron Smith, walked up and rescued Gary. Little did I know Ron would one day be my manager as well.

A few days later Renee and I walked into our house and found the light blinking on our answering machine. "Hi," the voice on the tape said, "this is Shawn McSpadden calling from Nashville. My dad, Gary McSpadden, met you Saturday night in Memphis at his concert. Clay, he loved your demo and brought it home for me to listen to. It's really good. There's a magical quality to your voice. We'd love to talk with you sometime about where you see yourself going in music. Please call me at your earliest convenience." Renee and I stood there looking at each other. We couldn't believe our ears.

"Play it again," she said. By the time the night was over, I must have replayed the tape fifty times. We jumped around, and Renee did a little victory dance. At long last someone from Nashville liked my voice. I called Shawn the next day and arranged a meeting in Nashville with him, his dad, and Ron Smith.

That meeting set in motion a chain of events that ultimately resulted in a recording contract with Reunion Records. But it didn't happen overnight. I made another demo that my dad financed and received more rejection letters. Renee and I moved to Nashville, although I didn't quit working for FedEx. They gave me a transfer, and I started working a day shift with my own delivery route. By day I delivered packages, and at night and on weekends I met with producers and sang wherever I could. I even auditioned with Bill Gaither for a spot in his vocal band. I didn't get the job, but Bill encouraged me to keep trying. He told me that eventually the right door would open.

I continued at this pace even after I signed on with Reunion Records and recorded my first album with them in Los Angeles. The label released my first single, "I Surrender All," a few months before my debut CD hit store shelves. The song started climbing up the charts while I was still driving packages around Nashville. Finally in April 1994, two years after Renee and I had moved to Nashville, I left FedEx and went on tour with Twila Paris and Phil Keaggy. My first CD, *My Place Is with You*, became the top-selling debut album of the year in contemporary Christian music, and "I Surrender All" hit number one on the charts. My unbelievable year was topped off when I won the Dove Award for New Artist of the Year. The dream that at one time seemed almost impossible had come true.

BE CAREFUL WHAT YOU ASK FOR

More albums followed, along with more number one hits. My concerts sold out, and my record sales soared. In the beginning, I would call Renee from the road and tell her, "Tonight I made as much in one day as I used to make at FedEx in a week." I stopped when my income level defied comparison with what I had earned in the past. It didn't take long for us to get comfortable with our newfound success. I thought this run would last forever. I genuinely believed my star would just keep soaring higher and higher.

As I look back on my climb to success, I can see that some sort of spiritual catastrophe was inevitable. Although I'd worked hard on perfecting my vocals, my spiritual life could not support the weight of success. I had too many cracks in my foundation. As far as God was concerned, I was still that seventeen-year-old boy keeping Him on retainer just in case I got into something I couldn't handle on my own. Sure, I prayed. At least I did while driving a FedEx truck and dreaming of stardom. Every day I asked God to put my demo tape into the hands of someone important. I asked for record deals and concert dates and everything else I needed to get discovered and become a star. When doors didn't open as quickly as I thought they should, my prayers turned into whines directed toward God. When it came to God, everything was about me.

By itself, my self-centered approach to God would have been bad enough. Combined with the sins lurking in my past, I was in serious trouble, and I didn't even know it. I'd kept my vow to walk away from pornography and never go back, but I'd never dealt with the problem itself. No confession to God. No repentance. No changes in my lifestyle to guard against temptation. I still believed the lie that pornography and everything it unleashed were nothing more than a temporary solution to the frustration I had felt over not being able to have sex before I was married. I mistakenly believed that because I was now married, the problem had solved itself. Yet the weight of my growing success would soon bring it back to the surface.

INTO MYSELF

As I progressed from ordinary working guy to successful recording artist, my focus became more and more fixed on myself. My career consumed me. I thought about it day and night. Even though I enjoyed a level of success, I wanted to push it even further. I wanted to be a star. I became convinced that in order to do this, I needed to be cool because cool sells. On stage and off, in interviews and on the bus, at home, at church, at the grocery store — wherever I was, I wanted to be more than some nerdy Christian singer. If given the choice, I preferred to do concerts in theaters and auditoriums rather than in churches because I figured they would be perceived as "real shows" rather than hokey church events. I wasn't into hokey. I was into cool. More than anything, I was into Clay.

On a purely human level, life was good, and Renee and I were happy. On the road, people constantly patted me on the back and told me how great I was. These constant strokes to my ego felt good. They felt *very* good. Throughout this time I kept sinking further and further into the pit of selfishness. I became this great star in my own eyes, and people fawning over me only made me more convinced I was right. Everywhere Renee and I went, people would do anything and everything they could for us. We would walk into a room after a concert or at a launch party for a record, and four or five people would bombard us with "Can I get you anything? Would you like a soft drink? Here's a tray of food for you." The lifestyle of a recording star, even a Christian recording star, only fed my appetite for more of me. With so many people wanting to serve me, I never thought of how I might serve other people. That was the last thing on my mind. I was too busy soaking in the fruits of my success.

For the first time in our lives, Renee and I had enough money that we didn't have to worry about how we spent it. And spend it we did. We bought a huge house, fancy cars, and designer clothes. We traveled and went out to eat whenever we wanted. That may not seem like a big thing, but it was for a couple of working-class kids from Memphis. We still went to church but only on Sunday mornings. Both of us knew God had given us this success, so we were generous with our money. If we saw someone at church in need, we tried to meet it anonymously. But our lives were still completely devoid of anything that might be mistaken for spiritual passion or discipline. Still, that never bothered me. I assumed that because God had so generously blessed our life, He must be pleased with the way we were living it.

Not only did we have lots of money, but we also had lots of free time. Too much time. I discovered that free time and excess money can be a deadly combination. As my career climbed, I did between 150 and 200 concerts each year. When I came home, I thought of my downtime as an opportunity to simply indulge myself with whatever I wanted. After all, I'd worked so hard to reach this level of success. At least that's what I told myself. When I was at home, I liked to just fall down in front of the television and start clicking through the channels. I've always been a movie fan, so Renee and I also spent a lot of time watching movies at the theater and at home. Some weekends we would go out to see as many as three or four movies and maybe watch as many at home. We didn't really care about the ratings. PG, PG-13, R, NC-17 — they were all the same to us. If Hollywood promoted a movie as a must-see film, we saw it. After a while we didn't have any standards when it came to entertainment. If it would amuse us, we watched it.

CROSSING THE LINE

Our viewing habits made it easy for me to justify watching pornographic movies again at the height of my success in 1996. After all, the content wasn't that different from the movies Renee and I were already watching. Mainstream movies have so much sex and nudity that you don't have to find a XXX video to experience pornography. Our standards had been so low for so long that I didn't see anything wrong with movies like *Striptease* or *Boogie Nights*. And moving from these films to the kind video stores keep hidden in a room in the back wasn't much of a stretch. I didn't feel that I was crossing a line because that line had been erased years earlier.

At least that's how I rationalized my reentry into the world of pornography. The truth of the matter goes a little deeper. When I watched a mainstream movie that contained graphic sexual content and nudity, something stirred inside of me. The old feelings I experienced when I watched pornography before I was married came back. I liked them, and I wanted more. As I said a moment ago, the focus of my life increasingly was me and what would make me happy. Pornography fed this hunger, and I knew where I could find it.

Now, I was no fool. There was no way I would risk being seen walking into an adult bookstore in Nashville to buy some videos. Someone would see me, word would leak out, and my career as a Christian singer would be over. Instead, I arranged for a friend to pick up a few videos for me. Like everyone else who surrounded me at that time, he was more than happy to get me anything I wanted.

Even though I told myself it was no big deal that I was watching pornographic videos, I didn't want Renee to know because I figured it would be a big deal to her. I told myself that women are funny about those kinds of things. We owned a huge home that had more closet space than our first house had floor space, so finding a place to hide the videos wasn't a problem. I also never watched adult movies on the pay-per-view channels in hotels while I was on the road. It would be too easy to get caught, and that could damage my career. Again, this didn't strike me as inconsistent with my rationalization that my new habit was no big deal. I told myself that not everyone was as enlightened as I was.

I lived this double life for nearly two years with hardly a pang of conviction. The years of casual Christianity had made my heart too hard to feel the Holy Spirit's touch. I could sit in church and hear sermons against sin without ever thinking I might need to make a change in my life. In my mind, watching people have sex on videotape was miles away from committing adultery myself. Not once did I stop and think about how I was poisoning my soul. To me, pornography was just another form of entertainment. I should have noticed it was something more when I started thinking about sex more and more often and my eyes began to wander toward other women. My life was on a collision course with disaster. It was only a matter of time.

4

THE LONG, SLOW SLIDE
INTO THE ABYSS

I didn't just wake up one morning and say to myself, *Gee, I wonder if I could get my hands on some pornography today.* My slide to this point came about very subtly. When my career took off and money started rolling in, I suddenly had the freedom to do anything I wanted. And I just wanted to have fun. You have to remember my spiritual condition at this point. My life was all about me. I kept God close enough for Him to whip out a giant umbrella to protect me from the storms of life, but far enough away that He couldn't tell me what to do. Renee and I still went to church. We even tithed, which seems strange when you think about how self-centered we both were. Life, to me, was all about having as much fun as possible and enjoying the ride.

My reentry into the world of pornography began with joking around with some friends. The jokes all had some kind of sexual bent and all of us laughed hysterically. Maturity-wise we hadn't progressed much from the high school locker room. The more comfortable I grew around these guys, the cruder my jokes became. I was simply repeating the type of humor I watched on cable all the time. To me it was a little on the edge, sort of risky, and very funny. Eventually I grew comfortable enough around one of the guys to start talking about pornography. We talked about how we used to watch it before we were married. Then I said something like, "So, you ever watch it now?" He gave me that guy look that says "of course" and something along the lines of, "Yeah, man, are you kidding?" Then I asked the question that pushed me over the edge. "Do you think you could get hold of a couple of videos for me? Don't worry," I said, laughing, "I'm good for the money. I'll pay you back." It was a short, simple, stupid conversation I shouldn't have had but one I'd wanted to have for a while. As I said in the last chapter, the mainstream movies I watched every weekend didn't leave a lot to the imagination. This seemed like the next logical step.

PORNOGRAPHY'S APPEAL

Even after my friend brought me a tape, I didn't watch it for a while. I guess maybe a part of my soul still had a small soft spot capable of hearing God speak. Or maybe a time when I could be sure Renee wouldn't walk in and catch me hadn't presented itself. To be perfectly honest, I've tried to forget as much of this as I can. If pornography wasn't such a problem for so many men, including men who profess to be Christians, I wouldn't write about it at all. Remembering those days is not a pleasant experience.

One day Renee left to go shopping for a few hours, and I found myself at home alone with nothing to do. So I dug out the videotape and watched it. I'm not going to lie to you. I liked what I saw. Later that night Renee must have thought I'd really missed her that afternoon because I couldn't wait to get her to bed. If you had asked me the next day if I felt guilty about what I'd watched the day before, I probably would have replied, "A little." I at least felt guilty enough not to tell Renee about the tape. But I couldn't see much of a downside at that moment. After all, the tape had sure spiced up things that night in the bedroom. What was the harm in that?

Those unfamiliar with pornography may wonder why its lure is so strong. After all, sex is sex. What's so appealing about watching a man and woman having sex? The physical act of a married couple and the couple on film is not so different, some might think, although one is right because it fits into God's plan and the other wrong because it does not. What's the difference, and why would anyone want to watch?

The difference could not be greater. In marriage, sex is an act of love. It is about becoming one, a real union. It is about caring. It is about serving. Sexual intimacy is an incredible and wonderful gift from God to a husband and wife who have committed their lives to one another. But in porn everything is about lust. It rarely shows one man engaged in a physical act with one woman, although it would still be wrong if it did because no one should be watching. Instead, porn shows two women together, or two or three women together, or two or three women with one man, or two or three men with one woman, and it goes on from there. It feels naughty. It is hot. It is heavy. It is raunchy. And it is sordid. These are obviously negatives, but men's carnal natures are very drawn to these things. This kind of sex doesn't feel like sex in marriage. It doesn't feel like same-old, same-old.

SLOW POISON

I didn't immediately feel the need to start watching porn every day. I would go for weeks or longer without watching any at all. So where was this horrible habit of mine? In my mind. Pornography, for me and I think for most people who are pulled into it, served as fuel for the lust fires inside of me. Maybe I just have a good memory, but I could replay the images in my mind over and over again. At first all I wanted to do was watch. That brought enough of a thrill. Sure, it kicked my sex drive into high gear, but I directed that toward my wife. If I had fantasies, they were always about Renee and me. Pornography simply gave them a little extra kick.

But over time, as these sordid images began to fill my mind, I started to put myself into them. The porn entertained me for a while, but eventually I started to ask myself, *I wonder what it would be like to be with two women at the same time?* As that question seeped into my thoughts, I started playing out that scene in my mind. Doing so gave me a huge charge. But with time the thrill started to fade, and so my fantasy life began to grow darker and darker. It was becoming a compulsion. My mind even began to think of Renee in various situations similar to those in the pornography I watched. I even got turned on thinking about her with another woman.

When I watched that first video in 1996, I did not think, *Oh, it would be a turn-on to see Renee with another woman or with another man.* If you had asked me about something like that, I would have been disgusted and sworn to you I would never, ever have such a thought. But porn is a poison that spreads into every part of a person's life. Because my wife was and is a huge part of my life, the poison changed the way I saw her as well. Eventually I began to think that I wanted our marriage to evolve into a very free, open sexual relationship in which she was with other people and I was too. If we were both okay with the idea, then it wouldn't be cheating for either of us.

How any man can think such degrading thoughts about the woman he pledged to love, honor, and cherish shows just how messed up I was. I was just sick enough to think that I would take her along on this ride too. I thought it would be fun, it would be hot, and she would like it.

THE POISON SPREADS

If God had not intervened, I eventually would have started acting out these fantasies and destroyed my relationship with my wife. These daydreams floating around in my head were not harmless fun. I didn't realize I was playing with fire. And the progression from watching porn as entertainment to hoping I would end up in a modern-day Sodom and Gomorrah did not take place overnight. The slide into the abyss of porn, lust, and sordid fantasies took place over the course of two years. By the end of those two years, I had made up my mind that I was ready to make my raunchy fantasies a reality. God stepped in before I physically crossed that line. If He had not, I shudder to think of where I would be today.

People ask me how Renee could keep from noticing all of this while it was happening. If she noticed any difference in our sex life, she probably thought, *Gosh, he's a wild man* or *He must really be crazy about me.* We had sex all the time before porn entered the picture, and nothing changed afterward. But as my fantasy life grew larger and larger, my sexual desires grew darker, and I moved further and further from her. Even though I had a beautiful wife who loved me and never withheld herself from me, I grew dissatisfied. Sex within the parameters of marriage as designed by God wasn't enough anymore. I started wishing for something more.

READY FOR DISASTER

I fell into this mess because I just wanted to have fun. That's all I really cared about. Even when I saw where this was leading, I didn't care because it felt good. That's all I really cared about. My pleasure. My desire. My lusts. Sure, I professed to be a Christian. After all, I meant it when I prayed that prayer all those years ago. But I didn't think about God too often. I thought only about myself.

Didn't Renee notice how far I was from the Lord and anything that might resemble a godly lifestyle? No, because sadly, she was as far from God as I was. Our sins were different, and she didn't know anything about the porn, but it wasn't a shock for her to hear me talk dirty or make off-color jokes around people because she did the same thing. Neither of us was living for the Lord. We were both so caught up in the world. My only secrets from Renee were my sexual fantasies and my pornographic videos. It wasn't that she thought I was godly; neither of us pretended to be that, at least not around each other. We were just living the high life. All the while we wore the tag of "Christian" and dragged God's name through the dirt. I'm ashamed I could ever have lived that way.

5

HE IS NOT SILENT

People have asked me if God ever spoke up during the two years that I slowly sank into the quagmire of pornography and lust. Usually I tell them I never heard Him because I was too busy enjoying the money and comfort my success gave Renee and me. At the time I thought God was saying something through the success. I thought He was telling me how pleased He was with me and how much He wanted to bless me. That sounds nuts, I know, but it also shows the deceptive power of sin. I became a pro at justifying my actions. Even in those moments when I knew what I was doing was wrong, I found some way to make it sound right. Remember, pornography wasn't the heart of my problem. The only thing I loved with all my heart, soul, mind, and strength was myself, not God. Pornography and pleasuring myself played right into this.

I might have continued on this descent into myself forever, but God loved me too much to let that happen. Proverbs 3:11-12 says, "My child, don't ignore it when the LORD disciplines you, and don't be discouraged when he corrects you. For the LORD corrects those he loves, just as a father corrects a child in whom he delights." Although I believed in Jesus, my actions denied Him. I thought I could just go to God when I needed Him, but He refused to play along. As my star was rising, I cared only about success, but God cared about me. I didn't realize it at the time, but He spoke in three unmistakable ways during my collision course with disaster. When I wouldn't listen,

He just waited a little while and turned up the volume until I couldn't ignore Him any longer.

MESSAGE ONE

Just as my career was beginning to take off, long before I crossed the line and started watching pornography again, God spoke through the mistakes of someone I looked up to as the model of everything I wanted to be in Christian music. In 1994, the year my first CD hit the stores, Michael English was the biggest name in Christian music. In that year alone, he won six Dove awards, including Artist of the Year. At the time, I idolized Mike. His voice influenced me like none other. A couple of years earlier I had met him when he picked me up at my house and drove me to my audition for the Gaither Vocal Band. Although I didn't get the job, Bill Gaither invited me to fill in for Mark Lowry on a few of the concerts Mark couldn't make. Those dates only confirmed my awe for Michael English. Standing on the stage singing with him and Bill Gaither was like a dream come true. After Mike left the Gaithers to start a solo career, I watched him closely. He was everything I wanted to be as an artist.

But Mike's life took an unexpected turn when, just one week after the 1994 Dove Awards, he admitted to having an affair with a Christian singer with whom he'd been touring. Their affair became public when the singer discovered she was pregnant with Mike's child. She later suffered a miscarriage. Ironically, they were touring to raise money for a shelter for unwed mothers. The news rocked the Christian recording business. Mike's label dropped him, and radio stations across the country refused to play his songs. He released a statement apologizing for his actions and announcing that he was withdrawing from the Christian music industry because of what he had done. He also returned his Dove Awards to the Gospel Music Association.

The scandal rocked me as well. Here was the guy I looked up to more than anyone else, and in one moment he lost everything: his home, his marriage, his career. All of it was gone because of sexual sin. I couldn't believe it. The scandal felt almost like a death had occurred in my family. He wasn't just some guy who fell. Mike had been my hero. His loss grieved me. Even though I didn't pray much back then, I prayed for him and his family. I kept wondering why he would make such a horrible decision and throw everything away right at the moment when he had it all.

After Mike's fall, *accountability* became the new buzzword in Nashville. People in the industry started talking about the need to surround yourself with people who would ask hard questions about your walk with the Lord. Mike stood out as the poster child for the perils of trying to go it alone, whereas being held accountable by people in your life can keep you from falling before it is too late.

All of this took place shortly after I left my job at FedEx to go on tour for the first time and a full two years before I fell once again into my own brand of sexual sin. First Corinthians 10:11 tells us to learn from the mistakes of others, and that's exactly what God was telling me through Michael English. At this crucial moment in my professional life, God planted a bright neon sign right in front of my eyes that said, "WARNING: DANGER AHEAD! Be very, very careful! Watch out for sexual sin! Get people around you who will help watch out for you!" But I didn't listen. I looked over at Renee and thought to myself, *I would never, ever do that to her. I would rather die than betray her.* At the time I thought that was enough. You already know it wasn't.

MESSAGE TWO

Two years after the Michael English scandal, as my career was flying high, my personal life was about to take a turn that would change me forever. And God spoke again, this time through Jim Fox. Jim and I grew up together and attended the same church. We knew each other pretty well, even though he was a couple of years younger than me. Jim had moved away from the Lord after graduating from high school, but God didn't leave him there. Around the time my first songs hit the radio, Jim rededicated his life to the Lord with nothing held back.

Once Jim got serious about God, he couldn't get enough of Him. He became a spiritual fireball. Every time I saw him, he wanted to talk about my music, but he didn't ask the usual questions. Most people asked about the latest news on my next CD or when I would go back on tour. Not Jim. He asked about the songs themselves. He would tell me how God used a song like "Time to Believe" to speak to him. Then he would always ask something like, "So is God doing the same thing in other people? What's going on in your ministry?" *Ministry?* I would think, *What ministry? I'm an entertainer!* I didn't sing in order to change people's lives. In fact, I really wanted to cross over out of the Christian market. That's why a lot of my songs had what I call "God or your girlfriend" lyrics that could be taken either way.

Just being around Jim caused me to feel instant conviction. He was on fire, and I wasn't. I was too busy being the cool, successful Christian recording star. He made me feel uncomfortable, but I spent so much time on the road that I didn't see him very often and was able to forget quickly any misgivings I had about where I may be headed spiritually.

One day in 1996, Jim came over to the house for a visit. His timing and the question he asked me could not have been coincidental. I had just crossed the line and started viewing pornography again. No one knew. No one. Jim and I were making small talk, just the two of us, when he looked at me and asked, "So, Clay, how's the lust factor?" *THE WHAT?* I screamed inside. *How did you know?* But I played it cool and said something like, "Well, you know, good days and bad. Ha ha. Hey, how 'bout them Yankees?" I don't remember the exact words. All I know is that I changed the subject as quickly as humanly possible.

I now see how God used Jim to reach out to me at a crucial moment. God knew what I had just gotten myself into. He wanted to pull me out before I sunk too low. Through Jim He gave me an opportunity to confess my sinful thoughts and get serious about my relationship with Him. I didn't take the hint, but God wasn't finished.

I found out a few years later, after my rededication to Christ, that Jim had been praying for me ever since that conversation. We ran into each other in front of a Walgreens, and he asked me how my life was going. Instead of dodging the question, I gave him an honest answer. I told him about how I'd sunk into pornography and lust and how God had pulled me out. But I didn't make it sound as though all my problems were behind me. I told him how I still struggle every day. I'll never forget what Jim did next. Standing near the front doors of a busy drugstore, he laid his hands on my shoulders and prayed for me.

THE FINAL WARNING

God kept warning me that my life was headed toward disaster, but I wouldn't listen. Over and over He pleaded with me to come back to Him. When I wouldn't listen to any of the voices God used to get my attention, He turned to one I had to hear: my own.

My breakthrough hit was a song called "I Surrender All," written by my good friend Regie Hamm along with David Moffitt. The song is amazing with its overpowering vocals. In many ways its message proved to be prophetic:

> I surrender all my silent hopes and dreams
> Though the price to follow costs me everything

> I surrender all my human soul desires
> If sacrifice requires that all my kingdoms fall
> I surrender all

I sang this song at every concert: 150 to 200 times a year from 1994 through 1998. But in spite of what the words said, I had not surrendered all to God. Not by a long shot. This song talks about giving control of every part of one's life to Christ. That was the last thing I wanted to do. Yet I still stood in front of crowd after crowd and sang the song as if I meant every word when really the only thing I cared about in that moment was hitting the right notes. *Words? What words?* I might as well have been singing in Swahili.

The third verse of the song is essentially a prayer giving God permission to strip away everything that keeps us from surrendering everything to Him:

> If the source of my ambition is the treasure I obtain
> If I measure my successes on a scale of earthly gain
> If the focus of my vision is the status I attain
> My accomplishments are worthless and my efforts
>   are in vain[1]

I didn't take the words of the song seriously, but God did. He gave me plenty of opportunity to change and to get my choices and life in order. Night after night, in one concert after another, He used my own voice to call me back to Him. And when I wouldn't listen, He took my voice away.

LIFE WOULD NEVER BE THE SAME AGAIN

Renee

6

THE BREAKING POINT

Clay's voice cracked as he tried to squeeze the words out over the phone. "It was horrible, Renee," he said to me as he broke into tears. "I just wanted to crawl off the stage and hide. What are we going to do?"

"It will be okay, Clay," I tried to reassure him. "We'll get through this, you'll see. This is nothing more than a temporary problem. Just give it time. Everything will work out." I tried to sound confident, but Clay and I both knew I was lying. Months had passed since his voice problems first surfaced in Savannah, Georgia. It wasn't that he'd lost part of his range. Clay could still hit the high and low notes, but he couldn't control the voice itself. It would give out and crack at the most inopportune moments. The problem hit at any point on his range, which meant it affected every one of his songs. Clay sounded tentative when he sang, his voice wobbly rather than controlled. He no longer had the commanding voice that landed him his record deal and pushed his songs to number one on the charts. I knew it. Clay knew it. And more and more, his fans knew it.

Clay tried going to doctors for answers, but all of them told him the same thing: There's nothing physically wrong. He tried to rest his voice as best he could, but the problem surfaced on the second night of a two-and-a-half-month, forty-four-city tour. Friends and other artists gave him all sorts of home remedies. Nothing helped. No matter what he tried, his voice still wasn't right. He couldn't count on it any longer. The two of us never talked about it, but both of us had already started contemplating life without music. The thrill ride we thought would never end had suddenly jumped the tracks, and neither of us was prepared for it. We loved the life of fame and success and comfort. If Clay couldn't sing, not only would we lose the life we relished, but we wouldn't even be able to afford the life we'd left behind when he quit FedEx. The future that seemed so bright just a few months earlier began to unravel.

WHAT A DIFFERENCE A YEAR MAKES

I never thought Clay and I would find ourselves in this position. Less than a year earlier it looked as if his career would shoot to even higher levels. In July 1997 Clay released what everyone thought was his best work to date, the CD *Stained Glass*. The music was more aggressive and edgier than anything he had done before. Clay even had a part in writing some of the songs. We held a listening party in our home immediately prior to the album's release. People from all over the industry gathered in our den to hear *Stained Glass* for the first time. Promoters, radio personalities, booking agents, journalists, record company executives, and some of our friends listened as Clay introduced each song. He shared what the songs meant to him and why he had included each on the album. Everyone's reaction blew Clay and me away. They were surprised he'd taken a huge artistic risk and released something so different from his earlier work. But they were also very impressed, just as we'd thought they would be.

The first two singles from the album, "He Walked a Mile" and "Saving the World," each shot to number one on the Christian charts. Clay had dreamed of joining the elite names in the industry such as

Stephen Curtis Chapman and Michael W. Smith. With the release of *Stained Glass*, it looked as though his dream would come true. That fall he embarked on an eighty-city concert tour promoting the new album. For the first time he had a full band behind him as he headlined the tour with Jaci Velasquez and Sunday Drive. The crowds loved him. Both of us could feel the momentum building. We could only imagine where we would go next.

THEN CAME SAVANNAH

Then Clay came down with a sinus infection when he was in Savannah. That in and of itself was no surprise as he usually gets one around the same time every year. He could barely talk, much less sing, but he went out on stage anyway. Singers have a creed that says they should try to sing through any problem, so he tried. When he called me later, he told me he couldn't believe how bad he had sounded. The promoters let the audience know he was sick to keep them from wondering why he sounded so unlike himself. I told him he needed to rest, but rest is a rare commodity in the middle of a concert tour. A local doctor prescribed antibiotics, and I hounded him to get plenty of liquids. By the time the tour ended and he came home to Nashville, he felt like his old self again. There was only one problem: His voice hadn't returned.

During his tour Clay had suffered another blow, this one to his ego and mine. *Stained Glass* had been completely ignored in the Dove Award nominations. Both of us thought this was hands down the best work he'd ever done, but apparently the Gospel Music Association didn't share our enthusiasm. Clay told me the news in a phone call from the road. I couldn't believe my ears. The first thought that flashed through my mind was *What will our family and friends think?* I immediately started looking for someone to blame. It had to be the record label or the promoters or maybe Clay's manager. Never once did it occur to me that God was trying to get our attention.

In the meantime, Clay's voice problems would not go away. I felt even more helpless than he did during this fight. Nothing I could say would help the situation, and most of what I said came out wrong. The more doctors he visited, the more depressed he became. A black cloud descended on our home.

Clay started going through huge mood swings, especially after concerts. When he was home he never wanted to leave our room. Some days he didn't even want to get out of bed. I thought he was losing it. After hearing one expert after another tell Clay there was nothing physically wrong, I started to think maybe the problem was in his head. Clay wondered if he would ever get his voice back. I wondered if I would ever get my husband back. The weight of these problems slowly but surely pulled him away from me and sucked him into himself.

With nowhere else to turn, I started to pray. Although I'd been a Christian since I was eight, I had rarely, if ever, prayed. Now my shallow spirituality came through loud and clear as I prayed, *Oh, God, You wouldn't really let my husband lose his voice, would You?* But as Clay's voice problem continued and his depression deepened, my prayers started to change. I started praying over Clay as he slept. Some nights I would also read Scripture passages over him. This was a radical step for me because I had never read the Bible outside of a Sunday school classroom. As Clay said, both of our Christian walks were pretty shallow. As I watched him struggle, I knew he was wrestling with some serious inner demons. At the time I had no idea how great those demons were. But one thing I did know: My husband needed God's help to survive this. Yes, I prayed for his voice to return. I prayed for this desperately. But I also started to pray that God would cover Clay with His love. In the name of Jesus, I would ask God to protect Clay's mind from Satan's influence.

Again, I didn't know everything that was going on in his life. God prompted me to do this. For the first time in my life, I learned what it means to really pray for someone other than myself. I did not yet know the work God was about to do in my marriage, but there I was, asking God to deliver my husband from problems I didn't even know he had.

HITTING BOTTOM

Clay's struggle reached a new low during a trip to World Vision's headquarters in Seattle. He'd been invited to sing for the organization's chapel service. Some of his friends from the industry were there, including the group Avalon. When he called me from his hotel afterward, I knew he had hit bottom. I should have prayed with him over the phone, but I didn't. Neither of us prayed very often by ourselves, much less together. However, as soon as I hung up, I started praying for my husband. The desperation in his voice worried me. *Oh, God, I don't think he can take much more of this. Please, please do something,* I pleaded. I fell asleep praying for Clay, and it felt as though I woke up doing the same.

When he came home the next day, I could hardly believe my eyes. He looked like a zombie. I asked him if he'd slept any the night before, but he just shrugged and went to bed without saying much of anything. I worried that he might be growing suicidal. The problem with his voice threatened to ruin his entire career, but I wondered if there was something more. He was, by then, an emotional and physical wreck. When he came home from Seattle, he started isolating himself from our family. His body might have been in the same house with our girls and me, but that was about it. He withdrew into our bedroom, and even when he came out, he wasn't there. Seeing him like this made me pray even harder.

I didn't know it at the time, but Clay made the connection between the problems with his voice and his out-of-control personal life during this trip to Seattle. In the first chapter he describes the conversation he had with God on the plane back to Nashville. During that flight Clay admitted to himself that his secret life of pornography and lust had deeply offended God. For the first time he started to see this habit for what it really was: a horrible, disgusting sin. Of course, at the time I didn't know any of this. All I knew was that the man I had known and loved for fourteen years was no longer the man living in my husband's body.

WHAT'S REALLY GOING ON?

Not long after the Seattle trip, Clay made one last-ditch effort to fix his voice problems. He went to see Chris Beatty, one of the best vocal coaches in Nashville. I noticed a change in Clay following his meeting, and it scared me. He was definitely not himself. Over the next few days he was very quiet and more distant than ever. At night he would excuse himself from the living room instead of watching television with me. "I need to finish up a few things," he would tell me as he went into his office.

On Friday night of that week we went out to dinner with our best friends. We had planned to see *Saving Private Ryan* afterward. All through dinner Clay sort of picked at his food and barely joined in the conversation. We always laughed at lot when the four of us went out, but not that night. Our friends looked across the table at me as if to ask, "How long has he been like this?" After dinner we drove to the movie theater and pulled into a parking spot. Before any of us could get out of the car, Clay said, "I just can't do this."

The rest of us looked at one another. "What's the matter, Clay?" I asked. "I thought you really wanted to see this movie. Is there something else you would rather see?"

"No, it's not that. It's just . . . " Clay's voice broke and tears started streaming down his face. His body shook. I thought he was having a nervous breakdown right there in the car. No one said anything. Our friends' eyes grew wide. They were scared for both of us. "I have a lot going on in my head right now and . . . " But Clay couldn't finish his sentence. He broke down in the car in front of our friends, and none of us knew what to do.

We drove back to our house, and Clay darted out of the car to the front door. Before getting out I told our friends, "It's his voice. The pressure is getting to him." But I knew it had to be something more. My husband wasn't just depressed. He'd changed. I started to wonder if I knew Clay as I thought I did. He seemed so erratic, so different. His behavior that night convinced me that he was on the verge of something, and I was afraid to think what it might be. The Christian music industry had just been rocked with several high-profile stars admitting to extramarital affairs. Walking into the house I thought to myself, *I wonder if we are next.* I wanted to ask Clay what had just happened, but I wasn't sure I really wanted to know. I wasn't ready to hear what he might say.

7

THE LONGEST DAY

A certain amount of craziness fills the house on Sundays, more so than on other days of the week. That Sunday was no different. Clay, the girls, and I woke up and got ready for church, just like we did every other Sunday morning. I went through the usual wrestling match with Savannah and Shelby as I helped them get dressed and then brushed their hair. At ten 'til nine we climbed into the car and drove to church, just as we did on most Sundays. After the usual round of smiles, waves, and small talk between the parking lot and the church building, we went to Sunday school. An hour later, we walked down the hall to the sanctuary for the worship service.

Everything so far said this would be a typical summer Sunday. That is until Clay leaned over a few minutes before the church service began and whispered, "We need to talk. Will you ask our friends if they can watch the girls so we can be alone?" I looked at him and muttered an okay, but I was anything but. The tone of his voice made it clear we weren't going to discuss changing the living room drapes. The fear that had hit me two nights before rushed over me.

"Can you tell me what this is about?" I asked.

"Not here, Renee. At home." He let out a sigh and then patted my arm as if to reassure me, but it didn't help. I looked over at him as the music started and wondered why he had picked this moment to say something like this. My mind flashed back over the past few months.

He had spent a lot of time on the road throughout the spring. Whenever he came home, he wasn't himself. I'd assumed his strange behavior was due to his voice problems. *What if that's not it?* I thought. *What if he fell for one of the girls working on his tour? It wouldn't be the first time that happened to a Christian star. Remember Mike English?* I tried to calm myself as the first worship song began. *Oh, God, please tell me my imagination is working overtime,* I prayed.

My head began to throb as I fought back tears. I could hardly breathe, much less sing or pray or hear anything the pastor had to say. After the service I loaded our girls into our best friends' minivan and started walking toward our car. My feet dragged across the gravel in the parking lot. I was in no hurry to get anywhere. When I finally reached the car, I opened the door, but I didn't get in at first. I didn't want to. I didn't want to go home. I didn't want to hear what Clay had to tell me.

Neither of us said a word during the ten-minute drive home. We just sat in silence as though the other wasn't there. Even as we walked into the house and changed into comfortable clothes, we didn't speak. Clay knew what was coming. All I could do was hope for the best as I feared the worst.

Clay walked to the family room, and I followed him. He took a seat on the couch, and I sat down on the other side of the room. It felt as if I was watching a movie I didn't want to watch. Once we were seated, he didn't ask if I was ready or anything like that. Both of us knew this was it. This conversation had to happen.

"Renee, you know I love you, don't you?" Clay asked. I nodded my head as he continued. "I know that God has blessed me so much with you and our girls, but now . . . " His voice trailed off. He swallowed hard, took a deep breath, and said, "But now I'm afraid I'm going to lose you."

Tears filled my eyes. I couldn't speak. *I'm right*, I thought to myself. I just knew the next words out of his mouth would be, "It's this girl. She worked on the tour with us. We got close and . . . " But they weren't.

Instead he said, "I'm really messed up, Renee. I have big-time problems, and I don't know what to do about them. I think my singing problems are due to a much deeper problem. I don't know how they are related, but I believe they are. You know how I've been freaking out about my voice. This has been the toughest thing I've ever had to face. I'm scared, Renee. I don't think my voice is ever going to come back. But that's not the worst of it."

Dread filled my heart as my mind screamed, *What? What!* On one hand, I didn't want to hear what Clay had to say because I knew our lives were about to change forever, but at the same time, he couldn't get the words out fast enough. *What is it, Clay?*

"I sense God is telling me that unless I change, I'm going to lose you, the girls, my career, everything. I'm in a bad place, Renee. I've sinned against God, and I've sinned against you." He paused and looked me in the eyes. Tears streamed down his face. I could tell he didn't want to keep going but knew he couldn't stop. "I'm out of control," he said. "My voice *and* my personal life are spinning out of control. Sexual lust is burning inside of me, and it is about to consume me."

With this admission, my worst fear suddenly swooped down on me. "I haven't had sex with anyone else," he said, which made me feel better until he said, "But I want to. I think about it all the time."

"Why, Clay?" was all I could say in response. "Why? I always thought we were happy together. What would make you want more?" I guess I could have started yelling at him and going ballistic. But I didn't. I was hurt and angry and felt completely betrayed, but I could see Clay wasn't lying to me. Nor was he making excuses. The longer we talked, the more broken he became, which, looking back, kept me from losing it with him. But I still had to ask, "Why would you ever think about sex with another woman, Clay? Am I not doing a good enough job here? You seemed happy every day with me. How did I fail? Aren't you satisfied with me?"

"It's not you," Clay said in response. "It's me. I have a problem, and the problem is lust."

Those words didn't help. They made me even more angry. "What?" I asked. "I don't understand. Is there someone in particular you feel attracted to?"

"No. No one. At least no one in particular."

His answer didn't make any sense until he told me about the videos. He said he wasn't looking at magazines or visiting adult shows or websites. Instead he was watching pornographic videos. At first I assumed this was something he did in hotels while he was on the road. I was wrong. He said he had a handful of videos hidden in his closet. He would watch them sometimes when the girls and I had left the house. At first, he explained to me, the videos were just like any other movie. But the more he watched them, the more he found himself fantasizing about the things he saw on the screen. His mind became twisted as he imagined himself doing sick things. Terrible things. He said he even wished he would find himself in a modern-day Sodom and Gomorrah with free sex everywhere. "Renee, I know Sodom and Gomorrah ended up completely destroyed. And that's where my life is headed if I don't change," he said.

I had no idea that Clay had been leading a double life. I couldn't believe the words coming out of his mouth. How could this be *my* husband with this problem? And how could I have not noticed? My mind couldn't wrap itself around what I'd just heard. Thoughts of divorce never entered my mind. Even with everything he'd told me thus far, I knew I would not give up on our marriage. Not because I knew that's what God would want me to do but because I was too proud. I didn't want to go through the shame of divorce. More than anything, I worried what everyone back home would think. I didn't want to live with that. I know how shallow that sounds, but it was all I had at the time. If Clay had named some woman with whom he'd had an affair, my reaction might have been different. But he hadn't crossed that line.

"This is really hard for me to understand, Clay," I said. "Are there specific women you want to have sex with? Is it someone we go to church with or someone on the tour bus with you?" My voice grew more intense with every question. I wanted names. If he had fallen for someone who worked for us, I would get rid of her. If it was someone at church, we would change churches.

Clay's answer was worse than I'd feared. He didn't want any woman in particular. He hadn't fallen in love with some other woman. It wasn't as if someone had come into his life and captured his heart. Instead, he burned with the desire to have sex with any nameless and faceless woman who would say yes. That fact frightened me even more. I wasn't competing with another woman but with every woman who happened to catch his eye. I thought, *He is absolutely out of control.* And I didn't know what to do.

"Is there someone around us you are attracted to and with whom you think about having sex?"

"Yes," he said.

"Who?"

"Anybody."

"So," I asked, "when we are at church and in our Sunday school class, you are looking around the room and fantasizing about the different women around us?"

"Yes," he replied. No explanation. No trying to shield my feelings with "maybe" or "perhaps." Instead he simply replied, "Yes."

I kept shaking my head. "I don't understand this," I said. "You must be sick. There has to be something wrong with you." He didn't argue the point.

"Let me get this straight, Clay," I went on. "You are telling me that if you had met a woman on the road who wanted to have sex with you, you would have done it?"

"Yes."

I just looked at him and said, "Are you kidding me? You would have cheated on me? You actually would have had sex with some woman you didn't even know?" And he said, "Yes." Not "Well, possibly." I think I wanted an "I don't know." "Yes" was almost more than I could take. "I don't know how you could think that," I said to him. "I don't know how you could want that. I don't know how you could hurt me like this."

He hung his head and replied, "I don't either." His eyes were red and his shirt was soaked with tears. I had never seen anyone so broken. He sat there weeping, crying out for forgiveness. At the same time, he prayed, asking God to forgive him and heal him. He confessed every one of his secret desires, even going back to those he'd had before we were married. He told me about the first time he'd seen pornography as a boy and how he'd hidden his porn habit from me during his college years. Listening to his confession, I was hurt and wanted to throw up. Yet, at the same time, I'd never seen anyone so broken over sin.

I stood up, shook my head, and walked to the kitchen. I poured myself a glass of water and took a long drink. As I turned and looked back toward the family room, I saw that Clay hadn't moved and knew he wasn't finished. He had more to tell me. This same scene played out many times over the course of the afternoon and early evening. I walked around the room firing questions, and Clay answered them. He did not try to cushion his response to spare my feelings. He was straightforward and brutally honest as he told me everything. He told me holding on to secrets was the last thing he wanted to do.

As hard as this conversation was for me, God gave me a glimmer of hope. Clay had changed. He didn't try to hide anything or make excuses. There were no "buts" following his admissions of guilt. He didn't try to shift the blame or excuse himself because of the pressure created by his career. Instead he told me everything he had done, all the secret thoughts, all the hidden lies. He wasn't proud of his actions. Far from it. He didn't have to say he was sorry for what he had done, although he did. I could see it in his slumped shoulders and broken spirit. He didn't come to me in search of sympathy. He pleaded for forgiveness.

First John 1:9 contains one of the sweetest promises found in the entire Bible: "If we confess our sins to him, he is faithful and just to forgive us and to cleanse us from every wrong." The word *confess* literally means "to say the same thing." The word goes beyond an admission of guilt. Anyone can admit he did something wrong, but that doesn't mean he wants to change. When we confess to God, we agree with Him about the nature of our sin. We see it the way He sees it, as something so disgusting, so repulsive that His only Son had to die in our place to save us from it.

That is what I saw my husband do as he confessed his sin to me and to God. When I share my story in conferences, women often come up to me and ask how I could forgive Clay so easily. I tell them I had no other choice. God had already forgiven him. What choice did I have but to do the same? I'm not making light of what Clay did. God didn't just brush his acts aside and say, "Oh, Clay, that's all right. After all, you are a man. I know how men are." The forgiveness Clay experienced came at the expense of Jesus' life on a cross. His grace swept Clay's sin away, and that same grace allowed me to forgive my husband and make a new start with him.

We talked for several hours until we were both physically and emotionally exhausted. I called our friends and asked if our daughters could spend the night with them. Neither Clay nor I were in any condition to try to act like mommy and daddy. We left the house and went to the movie we'd tried to see a couple of days earlier with our friends. Even though we sat in the dark theater and the movie flashed on the screen in front of us, neither one of us really saw it. Tears flowed until I couldn't cry anymore. I kept asking myself how we would ever fix this mess. And I wondered how we had allowed ourselves to get to this point in the first place.

8

TRYING TO KEEP MY HEAD ABOVE WATER

Clay's confession to me marked the end of his secret life, but it also marked the beginning of my having to deal with it. He told me that he'd thrown out his porn collection and that he was working hard to get his thought life under control, and I chose to believe him. He asked for my forgiveness, and I gave it to him. As I said in the last chapter, I'd never seen anyone so broken over sin. What choice did I have as a Christian but to forgive him?

However, none of this means that everything was suddenly perfect in our relationship or in our marriage. After his confession, a flood of emotions swept over me that I did not expect to feel. To be honest, I don't know what I expected to feel. Never in my wildest dreams did I think I would ever face something like this. I couldn't understand why my husband would turn to pornography and masturbation for satisfaction. Even though I'd forgiven him, I still felt betrayed and violated because of what he had done.

Over the next few weeks and months, I didn't know if I would survive. God's grace is the only thing that allowed me to get through it. By myself I never could have kept my head above water, not when every day brought a new wave of emotional pain.

INADEQUACY

Before Clay and I were married, I worked around women who told me, "Oh, the sex is great your first year, but you both get over it. You'll see." Every time they started in like this I would tell myself, *That won't happen to Clay and me. We're going to have a great sex life.* I was determined to meet all of Clay's needs and desires. We'd waited until we were married to sleep together, and I was going to show him that the wait was worth it, not just for the first night or the first year but for the rest of our lives. And I thought I had. I thought we had a great sex life.

Hearing my husband say he was on the verge of acting out with other women the sordid things he'd watched on those videos felt like a slap in the face. I took a lot of pride in our sex life, and now he told me it wasn't enough. My first thought was *Where did I fail?* Even though he told me over and over that the problem had nothing to do with me, his reassurances didn't help. I felt inadequate as a woman. "Aren't you satisfied with me? What more could I have possibly done? If you have great sex every day, how could that not be enough?" I wanted to know. Some days I would stand in front of the mirror and wonder why he would want to look at other women. I wondered if I should have dressed in a different way or maybe cut my hair short or grown it longer. I would turn to the side and wonder if I hadn't lost enough weight after our girls were born. Self-doubt overwhelmed me. *Something must be wrong with me.*

With time and God's help, I eventually came to see that the way I dressed and looked had absolutely nothing to do with Clay's problem. It had nothing to do with how well I was doing as a lover. I didn't drive Clay to porn. His flesh did. Sin did. (I've since observed that pornography and lust can strike any home. It doesn't matter a wife's age or appearance. I've had beautiful, young newlyweds as well as women in their seventies come to me in tears telling me that their husbands are hooked on pornography.) I know this now. I probably knew it then as well. But it took time for this knowledge to help me get past the sense of utter failure I felt as I thought about what Clay had done.

BETRAYAL

Even though I had forgiven Clay, I didn't know if I would ever be able to trust him again. He reassured me over and over that he had never acted on his desire to sleep with someone else. If he had, I don't know how I would have reacted. I had a hard enough time getting past his virtual adultery. I can't say what I would have done if he'd started naming names of other women he'd been with. This was bad enough. I felt as though Clay had taken not only the commitment we'd made to one another on the day we were married but all the promises we'd made to each another and stomped them into the mud. I felt as if I couldn't count on anyone or anything ever again.

This sense of betrayal made it hard for me to believe Clay when he said he was a different man. I wanted to believe him and tried to trust him, but a nagging thought haunted me: *If he can lie to you once, what makes you think he won't do it again?* When I left him alone at home, I would wonder if he had pulled out a hidden video and put it into the VCR. I tried to push those thoughts out of my head, but then I would find myself hitting "home" on my cell phone's speed dial. Clay would answer, and I would try to make it sound as if I just wanted to talk. Casually I would say something like, "So, what are you up to? Getting a lot of work done?" Ten minutes later I would call again. And again. And again. I thought to myself, *If he is watching porn, I'm going to make it impossible for him to enjoy it.*

I know I may sound a little inconsistent. How could I say I believed

Clay when he said he was through with porn yet call every few minutes to try to catch him in the act? I don't know the answer; I just know I did. The feelings of betrayal needed more than a few hundred "I'm sorry's" to go away. They made me question Clay's motives and wonder what he was really thinking, especially when we had sex. There were times when we were physically intimate that I wondered if he was replaying a porn scene in his head. Part of me didn't want to be intimate with him again, but another part of me believed that withholding sex from him would be counterproductive. Still, the thought of the things he had watched made my skin crawl, so I tried not to think about it. I didn't want him to close his eyes during sex because I didn't want him imagining he was with someone else.

The sense of betrayal put me on an emotional roller coaster. Some days these feelings became so strong that I couldn't bear to be close to Clay. He would touch me, and I would tell him, "You've got to give me some space because I'm in a pretty bad place right now." When the darkest days descended on me, Clay would do something he had never done before. He would pray for me. It was the best thing anyone could ever do for me. Prayer and clinging to promises I found in God's Word were the only things that got me through those days. I had always leaned on Clay, and he had let me down. During those black days, I discovered I could lean on Christ alone. He would never let me down. And He hasn't.

ANGER

Somehow, and I have to say it was by God's grace, I didn't scream at the top of my lungs or throw anything at Clay when he confessed his sin to me. I easily could have. After all, those would have been very natural reactions. But that is not to say I didn't become angry with him;

I did. I was so mad that I'm surprised smoke didn't come out of my ears. However, Clay's brokenness and honesty broke through my anger. When I told him I forgave him, I meant it. But that didn't mean my anger over this sin went away, never to return.

For months, Clay's betrayal was the first thing I thought about in the morning and the last thing that crossed my mind as I drifted off to sleep. Even as Clay and I made progress at rebuilding our marriage, I could not escape what had happened. Nor could I ignore this huge character flaw in my husband. I knew if he wasn't very, very careful he could fall again. These facts stared me in the face all day every day. I found myself thinking about them day after day and night after night for weeks and months on end. And I got sick of it. And it made me mad. I wasn't angry only about what Clay had done. I was also angry with him for making me think about this 24/7, for disrupting our lives in such a way that we could never go back to the way we were before. I would tell myself that this was all behind us, that Clay wouldn't do these things again, but that wasn't enough. There were days I simply wanted a little relief from the long, hard job of cleaning up this mess. But I couldn't find it.

With these thoughts constantly on my mind, I became hyperaware of the sexually charged material that surrounds us in this world. When Clay and I watched television, I noticed every sexy woman on the screen. I would glance over at Clay, and if his eyes seemed to stay on the screen too long, I could feel my blood pressure begin to rise. More than once I would get up, go to bed, and pretend to be asleep when he came in the room so he wouldn't get any ideas for the night. I wasn't so much mad at Clay as I was at whoever is behind the constant barrage of sexual images in our culture. These images are everywhere, and the sight of them would send me into a tizzy. More than once I went over to a magazine stand in the airport or grocery store and turned over every magazine with some sultry babe on the cover. I could have torn them all to shreds they made me so mad.

I wish I could say that the anger is completely behind me as I write this, but I can't. A couple of days before I started on this chapter, Clay sang at a youth rally. At the end of the night he went back on stage and shared his testimony. In the middle of the altar call he said, "I have to recommit my life to Christ every day. I still struggle with sin. I fell into pride today. I lusted today. . . . " Those last three words hit me like a punch in the stomach. They caught me completely off guard. I was sitting there, asking God to speak through him, and Clay said, "I lusted today." BAM! My head snapped up toward the stage, and I looked at him in disbelief. *What!* I screamed inside. Needless to say, I found it harder to pray during the rest of the service. He hadn't fallen back into his old, secret life. Clay was simply being honest about how vulnerable he is to temptation. Just as he will continue to fight his battle against the temptation to lust, I will have to fight my battle against becoming angry with him when his weaknesses are flung in my face.

GRIEF AND SHAME

During this time I lost about ten pounds. We had a family picture taken, which I now know was not a very wise thing to do. In it my eyes and cheeks look hollow, my smile forced. I never hung the picture where anyone could see it.

I've never shed as many tears as I did over those few months. In many ways it felt as if someone close to me had died. I guess he did. The image I once had of my husband as a knight in shining armor had come crashing down. The man I wanted to look up to and respect hadn't just disappointed me; he had descended to depths I never thought possible of him. I missed the man I'd thought I married. Turning loose of that image was a very hard thing to do, almost like turning loose of someone I loved who had died.

Along with the grief, I felt an incredible amount of shame. I wasn't as much ashamed of Clay and what he had done as I was of myself. I know it sounds crazy. The shame I felt came from deep inside myself. I just felt dirty. The pornography and lust had taken the beautiful gift of sex God had given us as a married couple and covered it with filth. I wondered if that part of our marriage could ever be normal again. I also felt ashamed when I thought of what people might think of me when the news got out. In my mind I could hear them thinking I was some cold prude who drove my husband to look for other outlets for sexual satisfaction because I wouldn't give it to him. No one may actually have thought such things, but this is how I saw myself. I wanted to curl up inside my house and hide from the rest of the world.

One day, when I felt as though I couldn't face another day, I came across Psalm 34:5, which says,

> Those who look to him for help will be radiant with joy;
> no shadow of shame will darken their faces.

This verse gave me hope when I needed it most. It told me God would help me if I would just look to Him. And that's where I had to turn. But that took a while. As you are about to see, when this crisis first hit, I was anything but ready for it.

UNPREPARED

Rick Warren begins his best seller *The Purpose Driven Life* with the words, "It's not about you."[2] Life, especially the Christian life, is not about our needs or our happiness or what we most want out of life. It's all about God. He made everything, owns everything, and is Lord over every part of creation. Life isn't about you or me. It is all about God and His Son, Jesus. He is to be first in everything. The apostle Paul put it this way:

> Christ is the one through whom God created everything in heaven and earth. He made the things we can see and the things we can't see — kings, kingdoms, rulers, and authorities. Everything has been created through him and for him. He existed before everything else began, and he holds all creation together.
> Christ is the head of the church, which is his body. He is the first of all who will rise from the dead, *so he is first in everything.* (Colossians 1:16-18, emphasis added)

In the first few days after Clay's confession, I realized I was not spiritually prepared to deal with it because up to that point I, like Clay, had built my life on the philosophy that said, *It's not about you because it's about me!* The indulgent lifestyle that Clay's success made possible allowed both of us to give ourselves everything we wanted. Even when Clay was still trying to break into the music industry, we never struggled financially. I never had to say no to myself about much of anything. I assumed that God wanted to make me happy, and I was. I believed that happiness and prosperity were signs of God's blessing on my life. My self-centered focus kept me from looking at God and putting Him first in my life. Jesus said that anyone who wants to be His disciple must first deny himself and follow Him (see Matthew 16:24). But I never did. I found my own self to be undeniable.

SATURDAY-MORNING JESUS

My Christian life didn't start out this way. When I was eight I came to Christ, thanks in large part to Hillie Roaten and his wife, Irma. Every Saturday morning the two of them would ride their bikes around Memphis neighborhoods, telling people about Jesus. They handed out suckers and candy to children, along with invitations to ride a bus to church the next day. My mother was a Christian, but my dad showed little interest in church or God. All that changed when he saw me get on the bus for Sunday school when I was only three. Dad started asking questions, and Mr. Roaten introduced him to Jesus.

I asked Mr. Roaten a lot of questions about God. His answers always explained what I needed to know in ways that I could understand. He didn't overwhelm me with information; instead he gave me the essentials a little bit at a time. He told me how our sin separates us from God and how Jesus died on a cross in our place. Those words stuck with me. Even as a child I knew I had sin in my life. Like every other little kid, I'd told lies and been mean to my sister. The more I thought about this, the more I realized I needed Jesus in my life. One night while lying in bed, I prayed and asked Him to forgive me and become my Lord and Savior. I called to my mother, who came into my room thinking I wanted another drink of water like I did every other night. Instead I told her, "I just asked Jesus into my heart!"

That moment has always stuck with me. Never once have I doubted that God heard my prayer and forgave all my sins that night. Nor have I ever been tempted to turn my back on my decision. I have always believed Jesus walked this earth and went through the same temptations we face yet never gave in to sin. I knew He died on a cross and rose again. I knew and believed with all my heart that He died for me, and I wanted to please Him. But ironically, I never thought about what it really meant to follow Jesus, other than by attending church and avoiding certain vices.

A PLACE OF REFUGE

From the time I was in seventh grade until I graduated from high school, my calendar was filled with church-this and church-that. I never found my place at school, but church was different. It was *the* place where I belonged. My friends and I hung out at the church gym on Friday nights, and I never missed regular services on Sunday mornings, Sunday nights, and Wednesday nights. Once a week teams from the youth group went into the community to invite people to Sunday services, and I went with them. I never said anything, but I was there. When it came to church, I was always there.

I had to go to church, but not because my parents forced me to attend. My compulsion came from deep inside myself. When I would have a horrible day at school, I couldn't wait to get home, get my homework out of the way, and go to church. Church was my safe haven, the place where I felt loved and protected. When I was sixteen, I started working at the Sears warehouse and came face-to-face with situations I didn't know how to handle. People would yell and cuss at me, and I would tell myself, *I just want to get out of here and get to church.*

Using the church as a hiding place from the world wasn't necessarily a bad thing, but I had allowed church to take God's place in my life. Church, not God and His Word, became my place of refuge, and consequently, my faith never grew up. Spiritually I stayed a little girl, running to safety rather than developing spiritual muscles. Even then my focus was on me. *My* needs. *My* happiness. *My* protection.

MISSING THE MARK

A few years after Clay and I started dating, he moved away to college. Without him I felt more isolated and alone than ever. Even though I attended a Christian high school, I didn't fit in. Our school had the same groups as every other school: the preps and the rich kids and the band geeks and the science nerds. I didn't click with any of them. On top of this, I was worried Clay would meet someone at college and forget all about me. I've always struggled with insecurity. If Clay even looked at another girl while we were dating, I would say something like, "So do you want to break up with me and go out with her?" Now, with him over two hundred miles away on what I was sure was a college campus crawling with pretty girls, my fears intensified and so did my sense of loneliness.

During this time I thought I was giving God what He wanted from me. I started every day with a quiet time and prayer and then continued praying throughout the day. But even though I prayed my way through the day, I never moved beyond a very self-centered type of Christianity. My prayers were always some variation of the same theme: *Oh, God, I feel so alone. Help me.* Although I turned to God in my moments of loneliness, I never allowed Him to use my loneliness to turn me away from myself. I simply wanted God to make me feel better. My world still revolved around me, even though God had a place in it. That's not biblical Christianity.

Following Jesus means considering other people as more important than ourselves and serving them with no thought of what we will get in return. Loving God means placing our focus on Him, His plans, and His desires rather than ours. Unfortunately, I was like many Christians I see today. I had it backward. We live and act as though God exists for us rather than the other way around. Even though we live good lives and do the right things, we still miss the mark. We may know the truth, but we don't really live it. At least that's how it was for me. I went to church every time the doors were open, prayed through school, and remained a virgin until I said "I do" at the altar on my wedding day. But that wasn't all God wanted.

No one had to tell me God wanted more. Deep down inside I knew it. I can remember driving to church during my teenage years and feeling overwhelmed with conviction. In those quiet moments God whispered, "You're really good at going to church and knowing about the Bible, but you aren't living this out on a daily basis." Tears would run down my face because I knew He was right. The words I allowed to seep into my vocabulary and my choices in entertainment didn't reflect Jesus. But it wasn't just that I was doing things that didn't reflect Him. He wanted to give me more of Himself, to draw me into a dynamic, personal relationship that went far beyond just showing up at church.

But instead of listening to His voice and asking Him to change me, I became well versed in justifying my actions. I muted the Holy Spirit's voice of conviction with excuses. After all, I was doing better than a lot of people I knew. So what if I said a cuss word or two? Everyone I worked with at the Sears warehouse cussed like sailors. What was the big deal if I said one or two choice words? The more excuses I made, the less I heard God's voice. With time, I stopped hearing it altogether.

AFTER WE SAID "I DO"

Once Clay and I were married, we settled into the typical American life. Clay had a good job at FedEx, and I went to work at a mortgage company. Neither of us intended for this arrangement to last the rest of our lives. Clay continued going to school at Memphis State, and I planned on leaving the workforce when we started having children. In the meantime, life was sweet. FedEx paid well and had great benefits, and because we didn't yet have children, our expenses were low. Both of us started accumulating possessions as we began our quest for success. We figured Clay would position himself in a career, advance as far as he could, make money, and buy nice things for us, and we'd eventually retire someday to a life of leisure. In our minds, that was what life was all about.

We knew better than to leave God completely out of the equation. We knew couples who had grown up in church only to abandon it after they moved out on their own. They found it easier to sleep in on Sunday mornings after a hard week than get up and spend an hour or two at church. We agreed that wasn't going to happen to us. Our church home had played a major role in our lives before we married, and nothing changed afterward. Because of our busy work schedules, our involvement shrunk down to whatever we could squeeze in on Sundays, but in our eyes, that was more than enough. At least we were there. We didn't drop out like so many others.

We were committed to attending church, but we weren't very committed to God, not in the ways He asks of us. Even after Clay started ascending the ladder of success as a Christian singer, we remained spiritually lukewarm. We simply transferred our goals for success to a new career path. Neither of us ever made a conscious decision to minimize God's role in our lives, which is one reason we didn't recognize that we were sliding down a slippery slope.

10

LOW STANDARDS, LOWER EXPECTATIONS

always thought Clay and I had a very open, honest relationship. We'd known each other for so long that I didn't think either of us could keep a secret from the other for any length of time. After dating for six years and being married for eight, we could complete each other's sentences. In my mind we were more than husband and wife and more than lovers. Our lives had been wrapped up in each other for so long that I believed we were one another's closest friend and confidant. The very idea that one of us could live a secret life apart from the other struck me as absurd.

So how could Clay watch pornographic videos for two solid years without my knowing anything about it? Obviously I didn't know my husband as well as I thought I did. How did I miss every warning sign?

The answer embarrasses me.

I loved the lifestyle of fancy houses and cars and everything else money could buy. My flesh couldn't get enough. For the first time in my life, I had everything I ever wanted. I was so caught up in myself and in the life of being a star's wife that I didn't notice a lot of things in those days. And the standards we set for ourselves didn't help.

LOW STANDARDS

When Clay and I were dating, we often got into fights at the movie theater because of the sexual content of a movie. I didn't want to see films that included nudity or any sexual content whatsoever. But as the years went by, my standards became more and more lax.

We got cable after we bought our first house, and my moments of moral outrage at the raunchy content of shows on HBO and Cinemax became much less frequent as I desensitized myself. With time, the type of humor I enjoyed became more and more coarse. I didn't just watch the crude routines on cable; I could recite them back to our friends line for line. (We didn't have much trouble finding friends who shared our indulge-yourself-because-grace-is-cheap approach to the Christian life.) All the while I told myself that the commitment I made to Jesus when I was a child protected me from any negative consequences resulting from the things I watched on television. (Did I mention that I never read my Bible during those years?)

My standards gradually declined until we didn't have any kind of moral filter for our entertainment choices, nor did we want one. We came to see ourselves as particularly enlightened and open-minded, as opposed to those legalists who wouldn't go see a great movie just because it might have an R or NC-17 rating. While I would never have told Clay I approved of pornography, participating in viewing movies with graphic sexual content said otherwise. I once even bought him a *Playboy* magazine because it featured Farrah Fawcett reprising her pose from a poster Clay had in his room as a teenager. I did not realize then the kinds of effects graphic sexual content can have on a person's soul. When scenes heated up in the mainstream movies we watched together, I always assumed any lust they might incite within Clay would be directed toward me. This was a foolish assumption.

Our standards hit rock bottom during a weekend getaway. The two of us were staying in a rented condo. While we lay in bed, Clay started flipping through the channels just to see what was on. This particular resort came equipped with every satellite channel you can imagine, including those that show adult movies. We soon found one. Both of us laughed, and I said something like, "Can you believe they would show *that* on television?" But Clay didn't change the channel, and I didn't ask him to. I could tell he liked what he saw, so I didn't put up a fuss. I knew we shouldn't be watching an adult-movie channel, but I justified it by telling myself, *It's just the two of us here. It may even spice things up. No big deal.* Besides, the overall content wasn't that different from my favorite soaps. The adult channel just left much less to the imagination.

MISSED SIGNALS

The low standards Clay and I shared did not cause Clay to start viewing pornography, but they made it much easier for him to justify it. They also kept me from noticing subtle changes I should have seen. Clay's talk became much more graphic and loose, both inside the bedroom and out, and he wanted me to join in. This didn't shock me because of the shows and movies we watched on cable, but I should have come to the conclusion that there might be something more. He also made suggestions of new things he wanted to try in the bedroom. Never did he suggest anything perverse or degrading to me, although I should have wondered what triggered his imagination. He also became much more aggressive sexually. I don't mean this in a bad way. Clay was on the road a lot. I simply took his aggression to mean he missed me after being gone for a week.

While these signals really only stand out in retrospect, there were a couple of other changes in Clay that I should have immediately jumped on. Over time he started making comments about the way other women looked. When an actress would come on the screen, he would say something like, "Wow, she's really hot!" The way he said this made it clear he was doing more than commenting on the way God made this woman. I could hear a real attraction in his voice. With time, these comments came with greater frequency and not just about women on the television screen or magazine covers. His eyes started roaming even when we were together.

I remember one day in particular. My girlfriend and I were about to leave a store when a very attractive woman went out the door in front of us. Clay and my friend's husband were sitting on a bench just outside the store waiting for us. I nudged my friend and said, "Watch this." Just as I expected, both Clay and her husband nearly broke their necks staring at the young woman as she walked by. She and I laughed, went over to our husbands, and said, "Shove your eyes back in your heads, boys. Your wives are back." The four of us had a good laugh and went on our way.

That's how I handled such incidents. I made jokes about them, and I lied to myself. I told myself that I was overreacting, that my old insecurities were acting up again, and that I was just being a prude. I should have said something, but I didn't, perhaps in part because this was the kind of behavior I'd grown to expect from men.

LOWER EXPECTATIONS

Prior to the changes God made in Clay's life and mine, I attributed these kinds of incidents to the nature of a typical male. I didn't like it, but I told myself that all men like to look at women. After all, that's how they are wired — they can't help it.

90

I got this impression early on. When I was a girl, I saw some of my male relatives staring at women as they walked by. Some of them even claimed to be Christians, but that didn't stop their eyes from tracing every curve on a woman's body. When someone questioned it, they would quip, "What's wrong? Where's the harm in looking?" Then when I went to work at the Sears warehouse as a teenager, this view was reinforced. All day every day, the guys I worked around not only stared at any female within half a mile, but they barked out sexually graphic comments and then laughed and slapped each other on the back. I heard what they said about every woman in the place, including me. If one of us got angry or complained, the guys would pass it off, saying something like, "What's the matter? Can't you take a joke?"

So when I started seeing the same behavior in Clay, I dismissed it as "boys being boys." I didn't have higher standards for him because I didn't expect any guy would ever be anything more than a sexist jerk. I should have expected more, especially out of a man who claimed to follow Jesus, but I didn't spend much time around anyone I would describe as completely sold out to Christ. I preferred the company of people like Clay and me: those who didn't see anything wrong with the movies we watched and the jokes we told. I rarely saw examples of true godliness in a male because in those days, most of the people we surrounded ourselves with lived by the same standards as we did. Most of the men acted just like Clay did. As a result, I tolerated behavior that I should have immediately confronted.

All of this worked together to create the conditions for a spiritual perfect storm. Low standards combined with lower expectations set the stage for the crisis that would change our lives forever. In many ways we put ourselves in this position together. I didn't push Clay to porn, and if I had discovered his habit on my own, I would have been hurt and angry. But by sharing the same low standards, lukewarm spirituality, and low expectations, I made it much easier for him to sink further into the abyss. Once I found out about it, I knew he wouldn't be able to get out of it alone. Nor could either of us repair the damage porn inflicted on our marriage by ourselves. It would take a team effort. We had to tackle this challenge together.

CLIMBING OUT OF THE ABYSS

Clay and Renee

11

REBUILDING TRUST

It looked as though we had it all: success, what appeared to be a happy marriage, two wonderful daughters. From the outside we looked like the ideal Christian family. And then this happened. We faced two daunting challenges. First, we had to disentangle ourselves from the tentacles of pornography. Second, we had to repair the damage it had wreaked in our lives. We didn't get to this place overnight, and fixing it was not easy. We felt a little like storm victims who have finally been allowed back into their hurricane-ravaged neighborhood. Looking at the extent of the damage and the enormity of the task was almost enough to make us throw up our hands and give up. Where does anyone start fixing something like this?

With so much to do, we knew there was one thing we had to take care of first. We had to bridge the gulf that porn and the pain it inflicted had spawned between us. That meant we had to reestablish trust between the two of us. No relationship can last without trust, especially a marriage. It forms the very foundation of the marriage covenant. Without it the two of us would essentially be working on our own, all the while casting a wary eye toward the other, wondering what was really going on over there. Neither of us could survive this without the other, and we wanted to do more than survive. We wanted to get over the past and chart a course toward the future God had in store for us and our marriage. To do that we needed to rebuild the bond of trust that had been broken. That meant we each had to make some difficult choices.

CHOOSING BROKEN HONESTY (CLAY)

Before Renee and I could move forward and repair the damage inflicted by the past, I knew I had to come clean with her about everything I had done. I couldn't simply get rid of the porn and start living for the Lord without telling her what had happened. She might have seen the change in me, but the secrets of the past would have created an ever-growing chasm between us. The Bible says husbands and wives are one flesh. In marriage, two become one body. Because of this, I knew I couldn't continually hide something from my wife any more than my right hand can keep a secret from my left. I suppose I could have in theory but not if I hoped to have anything approaching a healthy relationship.

I needed Renee's forgiveness. In the Bible, when people got right with God, they immediately went and set things right with the people against whom they'd sinned. Zacchaeus, a tax collector, is the classic example of this. After he decided to become a follower of Jesus, he sought out and paid back the people he'd cheated (see Luke 19:1-10). I needed to do the same to the one I'd cheated. Seeking Renee's forgiveness forced me to open up and become completely transparent with her. She needed to see that I had nothing left to hide, that I wasn't holding on to secret sin any longer. And she needed to see how I really felt about what I had done. If I'd made excuses or been anything but completely broken over my actions, my cry for forgiveness would have been a fraud.

I didn't choose just to confess. I chose to become transparent before my wife, not only about my past but also about the present. Even now, I do not hide my daily struggles from Renee. I can't lie to her because she will see right through me. I wish I no longer felt tempted, but I do. I know I will wrestle with this same temptation for the rest of my life. When I do, I tell Renee about it. I don't tell her to hurt her. Far from it. I tell her to seek her help. A marriage isn't two perfect lives coming together. It's two normal people being real with each other and sharing their lives, both the good and the bad. This honesty is what trust is all about.

THE DECISION TO FORGIVE AGAIN AND AGAIN (RENEE)

When Clay first confessed his sin to me, I felt everything any normal woman would feel. Anger. Resentment. Hurt. More anger. I could feel my spirit tightening up and closing off from him. In the days and weeks that followed, he continued confessing things from the past that he had neglected to confess during the first go-around. Every time he came to me with something new, it felt like a fresh blow against a broken arm. More hurt. More pain. More anger. Each time my spirit would tighten up. I was like an emotional turtle. I wanted to pull back into a shell to keep from being hurt again.

But the way Clay confessed each time made it easier for me to forgive him. He never confessed like some hardened criminal acknowledging that he'd been caught. He was genuinely filled with sorrow over everything he'd done to me. Even the first time he confessed his secret life to me, his brokenness convinced me I had to forgive him. Each time I chose to forgive Clay, God's healing touch swept over my soul, allowing me to do something I never thought I could do. I could once again open up to Clay and make myself emotionally vulnerable to him. More than that, forgiveness bridged the pit of his sin and brought us back together. Until and unless I forgave Clay, a wall of distrust and anger would always separate us. The simple words, "I forgive you," repeated over and over again, allowed the process of rebuilding trust to begin.

CHOOSING PATIENCE (CLAY)

I never assumed one afternoon of confession would fix everything in my relationship with Renee. My actions hurt her deeply. She forgave me, but the emotional wounds wouldn't disappear overnight. Neither would the anger and the doubts and all the other emotions my confession unleashed in her. She needed time to work through them all, and she needed time to learn to trust me again. I told her I had changed, but only time could prove I meant what I said. I had to give it to her. I had to be patient. Very patient. Without it our relationship could not be rebuilt.

I wanted Renee to trust me again, but because of what I had done, I wasn't surprised when she called nine or ten times during a trip to the grocery store the week after my confession. It would have been easy for me to get irritated or to yell something like, "I told you I have changed! Why won't you believe me?" But she didn't need that. I had to be calm without complaining or becoming irritated with her.

Throughout this time of healing, we would hit days when it felt as if we'd taken two steps forward and three steps back. One of us would find ourselves in a "dark place," which was our code term for those days when we felt as though we were drowning in the past. Renee didn't have to say anything when she found herself losing her struggle with the pain I'd caused. Her actions showed it. Or rather, her reactions. I would touch her arm, and she would bristle. Or I would ask her to pray with me, and she would refuse. "I'm in a dark place right now," she would tell me, which let me know she was revisiting everything I had told her and was having a hard time dealing with it. Again, I could have said something cold like, "Come on, Renee. It's been months. Get over it already." But what good would that have done? Yes, I'd changed. And yes, I wanted our lives to get back to normal. But I couldn't rush the process. She needed me to be patient, not argumentative.

When Renee has a difficult day, I don't lecture her or become angry. I may want to, but giving into this temptation always ends in trouble. Instead, I simply pray that her spirit will open back up. She's told me that there are times she wants to tell me, "You know what, buddy? I don't want your prayers right now!" I've never heard her say this in so many words, but I can see it in her eyes and in her reaction to my touch. But I go ahead and pray over her anyway. I pray for her emotional healing and for God's grace to touch her life and mine. He always comes through.

THE DECISION TO RELEASE MY FEARS TO GOD (RENEE)

After Clay told me he'd fantasized about having sex with other women, my old fears and insecurities came back to haunt me. Even though Clay struggled with his voice, he kept on singing. His career didn't end, which meant he had to continue going out on the road for concerts. And that's when my fears grew to a fever pitch. All kinds of what-ifs kept running through my head the entire time he was away from home.

What if he finds himself face-to-face with a Playboy *magazine while buying a newspaper at the airport newsstand?*

What if a woman sits down next to him while he's waiting for his plane, and she starts flirting with him?

What if Christie Brinkley is next to him on the airplane?

What if some woman goes to his hotel room and throws herself at him? I knew this had happened to other artists. What if it happened to

Clay? What if? What if? What if? I tried to squeeze the thoughts out of my head, but they wouldn't go away. I was working hard to trust Clay, but I knew temptations would come looking for him. I felt helpless, and my fears would not go away.

In the middle of one of my what-if worry spells, I suddenly realized I had to surrender my fears to the Lord if Clay and I were going to make this marriage work. My fears made me distrust Clay. After all, he'd already let me down once. But I knew I could trust God. He's never let me down, and He never will. I had a choice to make. Either I could worry and wonder and allow myself to become an emotional wreck, or I could trust God and pray. I chose the latter. I told God, "Lord, You know all these terrible thoughts running through my head. I can't do anything about them, so I give them to You." Instead of allowing the worst-case scenarios to continue to play in my head and consume me, I used them as promptings from God to pray for Clay and seek the Lord's face. The more I prayed and surrendered my fears to God, the more my fears evaporated and the closer I grew to Him. What a wonderful trade!

The Spirit prompted me to pray for Clay every day, and I continued to pray for him when he was asleep. I would use a passage from the Bible as a guide for my prayers. Proverbs 22:3 became one of my favorite verses to pray for him. It says, "A prudent person foresees the danger ahead and takes precautions; the simpleton goes blindly on and suffers the consequences." I would ask God to open Clay's eyes to the dangers ahead and to help him anticipate situations and people he needed to steer clear of. I prayed that he would see trouble coming long before it arrived and that God would help him get out of its way.

Releasing my fears to God also diffused the anger that kept coming back. The more I prayed for Clay, the more I discovered that I cannot stay mad at someone for whom I am praying. At least not for long. As

I prayed for Clay, a freedom from the past swept over me. Love and forgiveness took the place of my anger.

THE DECISION TO TURN LOOSE OF THE PAST (RENEE)

I'm a detail person. I want to know everything. In the days and weeks immediately following Clay's confession, I felt I needed to know everything he was thinking. Questions popped into my mind about specific people and situations in our past, and when I asked Clay about them, he always answered with the same honesty he showed on that Sunday afternoon. Some days I didn't even have to ask. Because Clay wanted to be completely transparent with me, he confessed any details he might have forgotten to tell me before.

At first I needed this. However, I finally reached a point where I'd had enough. Listening to my husband's confessions of weakness was not easy. One Sunday one of our girls woke up feeling sick, so Clay went to church without me. When he came home, he told me that an attractive woman had sat down across from him. He started feeling tempted, so he got up and moved away. My initial thought was, *I can't believe you are so weak you can't sit in a one-hour Sunday school class without being tempted!* But I didn't say that. Instead I asked, "So did you sit there and lust after her?"

"No. Absolutely not," he replied. "I didn't let it get to that point, Renee. When I felt myself being tempted, I ran from the temptation rather than giving in."

Then it hit me. Instead of being angry that Clay had been tempted, I needed to rejoice that my husband was now a different man. That morning the Lord told me to turn loose of the past and focus instead on the man in front of me. I have to see my husband for who he is today. In the past he let lust consume him. Now he values holiness above everything else. He still feels tempted, but how can I hold that against him? Even Jesus was tempted. Temptation is not sin. Giving in to temptation is.

Understanding this truth allowed me to choose to trust Clay even as doubt tried to descend upon me. He is not the same person who stashed pornography in his closet. The man who could not be trusted doesn't live here anymore. God changed Clay into a man who longs to know his Savior and to please Him in everything he does. When I turned loose of the past and instead focused on the work God is doing in my husband's life, I could start to trust him again without fear.

Releasing the past is easier said than done, but rebuilding trust demands it. When we forgive, we do not lose the ability to recall the past. It's not like deleting files from a computer. In fact, we shouldn't forget what brought us to this point in our lives. But instead of allowing the past to become a wedge between Clay and me, I let God use it as a reminder of the greatness of His power and grace. Rather than pulling up old episodes and hammering Clay with them, I allow those memories to become road marks that remind both of us how far we have come in our journey with God.

GO FORWARD WITH A CHANGED LIFE (CLAY)

I couldn't just talk about how I was through with porn and how I wanted to live a new life. I actually had to do it. The apostle Paul put it like this: "I preached that they should repent and turn to God and prove their repentance by their deeds" (Acts 26:20, NIV). Renee had to see a different man if we were truly going to go forward. I couldn't undo the past. No one can. But I could change the future. Once I knew we were on the same team, working toward the same goal rather than fighting against one another, I could start that process. And it all began with the simple act of repentance. My life as a man and our life as a couple had to go in a radically different direction than the direction we'd traveled during our first eight years of marriage.

12

U-TURN

Pornography was a huge problem that almost wrecked our marriage. Because of it, trust was broken, vows compromised, and the very heart of the marriage covenant threatened. Repairing the damage it caused took us years. And yet, as we've said, pornography wasn't our biggest problem. If we had tackled the problem of porn but neglected the larger sin, our home might have survived, but we really wouldn't have been any better off. But by addressing the larger problem, we discovered an essential step toward solving the problem with pornography. The first thing we had to do to climb out of the pit of pornography was turn around. We had to stop living for ourselves and instead live for the Savior we both professed to love and follow.

A CHANGE OF MIND (CLAY)

Although I rationalized my behavior, I knew viewing pornography was wrong. I knew it the first time I saw it when I was a boy. I knew it when I hid magazines in my room in high school. I knew it when I went to the adult theater with one of my buddies in college. And I knew it when I asked a friend to buy me a couple of videos from an adult bookstore in 1996.

But I never wanted to admit this truth to myself. Instead, I dismissed what I did as no big deal. I told myself watching porn was no different than watching the Pittsburgh Steelers play football. Even as the fire of lust started consuming me, I lied to myself about what was happening. I told myself that even if I crossed the line, I still loved Renee too much to leave her, and my marriage meant too much to me to ever seek a divorce. For some reason I never stopped and asked the next logical question: If I loved Renee so much, why would I contemplate committing adultery?

Obviously, I had to stop lying to myself and admit what I already knew was true. My actions were wrong. Dangerously wrong. In the Bible, confessing a sin means more than admitting guilt. It means we see our actions from God's perspective. God pried my eyes open in the days between my trip to Seattle and my visit with Chris Beatty. He refused to let me ignore the true nature of my actions any longer. I wanted to say that the fantasies running through my head were nothing more than harmless fun. God showed me they were the spiritual equivalent of breaking the sixth commandment. He swung my head around to see His Son hanging on a cross with my sin driving the nails deeper and deeper into His hands. The sight horrified me.

Three of my biggest hits talk about the Cross of Christ and the power of His blood: "He Walked a Mile," "The Blood Will Never Lose Its Power," and "Saving the World." I sang about the Cross, but I'd never seen it for what it really is. The whole time I justified my porn habit, I also carried around this idea that it didn't really matter what I did because Jesus would forgive me. My self-centered, casual approach to God used the Cross as my carte blanche to keep on sinning so that grace could increase (see Romans 6). Everything changed when I saw how my sin had nailed Jesus to the cross. I was personally responsible for His death. I wasn't just guilty of watching some video I shouldn't have watched. I was guilty of putting the Son of God on the cross.

As I stumbled to the foot of the cross, I not only came face-to-face with the magnitude of my sin, but I also experienced the incredible power of God's love and grace. Looking up into the eyes of Jesus, I felt His love sweep over me. I broke down and confessed what I had done, and He forgave me. From that moment on I knew I had to live only for my Savior. I say "from that moment," but in truth this whole process took place over time, from the plane trip home from Seattle to Chris Beatty's studio to our family room with Renee. When I finally repented of my sin, the direction of my life changed.

A SINGLE PASSION (RENEE)

As Clay and I tried to crawl out of the hole we'd dug for ourselves, I faced many days when I thought my strength would give out. Neither of us knew how all of this would turn out although both of us were determined to do everything we could to fix our home. In the midst of the nightmare I just wanted some peace. My heart ached for it.

I also needed wisdom and counsel. I felt like a little girl who wanted nothing more than to curl up in her daddy's lap and feel his arms wrap around her. I didn't know how to help my husband. I needed someone who would listen when I vented without acting shocked and would then offer advice without making me feel like a total failure.

More than anything I needed hope. I needed the reassurance that our problems were not insurmountable and that somehow our marriage would not only survive but would thrive on the other side of this mess.

Then I came across Isaiah 9:6, which describes Jesus' character more than seven hundred years before He was born. It says, "For a child is born to us, a son is given to us. And the government will rest on his shoulders. These will be his royal titles: Wonderful Counselor, Mighty God, Everlasting Father, Prince of Peace." As I read this verse, I realized Jesus alone offers what I was searching for. I needed peace. He is the

Prince of Peace. I needed wisdom and counsel. He is the Wonderful Counselor. I needed a place of refuge. He is the Everlasting Father whose love never ends. I needed hope. He is the Mighty God who is far greater than any problem we can throw at Him. So that's what I did. I threw my problems at Him. He didn't mind. In fact, He tells us to throw all our cares His way. First Peter 5:7 tells us, "Cast all your anxiety on him because he cares for you" (NIV).

All through my adult life, I sought success and comfort and all the shiny things this world offers. But they weren't enough. When I thought my marriage might end, the fame and success didn't matter anymore. In the beginning I turned to God out of desperation. But as I prayed and sought the Lord, I made an amazing discovery. The more I learned about Jesus, the more I hungered for Him. In the midst of those dark days, God awakened within me a passion for Him.

Both Clay and I began to pursue God as we never had before. We didn't just start reading our Bibles and praying together. Both of us got excited about God. It was as though we could not get enough of Him. We'd spent our whole lives in church and had heard the truth all through that time, but it felt as if we were discovering God for the very first time. Clay would come home, and I would corner him and say, "You will not believe what I discovered today!" Then I would read him some passage of Scripture I'd read and say, "Wow! Isn't that *great*?" The Scriptures became more than ink on a page. I could hear God speak to me through them as if He were standing in the room with me. He became so much more personal, so much closer than I'd ever experienced. Before this, I'd always just counted on God to meet my needs and bless my life. Now I realized that my greatest need was to know Him, and the greatest blessing came as I lost my life in His. This passion for the Lord became the driving force within our home.

SURRENDER TO GOD'S PLAN (CLAY)

You might assume that once I heard what God was trying to tell me by taking away my voice, He would give it back to me the way it was before. He hasn't. The voice you hear in my old hits such as "I Surrender All," "My Place Is with You," and "The Rock That Was Rolled Away" has never fully returned. I cannot sing those songs exactly as I once did. I've prayed and asked God to restore my old voice, but He hasn't. My friends in the industry have even laid hands on me and prayed over me. More than seven years have passed, and, while I've seen improvement, the voice that caught Gary McSpadden's attention is now different and may never return to what it once was.

It's easy to follow God when He is fixing the mess you have made of your life. But what happens when He doesn't do what you expect or want? The real test of whether the direction of my life had truly changed came when I did what God asked but still didn't get my voice back. Was I serious about this U-turn when God didn't fix everything but instead told me to trust Him because He knows what He is doing? Would I surrender to God's plan, even when it took me somewhere I didn't want to go? I realized I couldn't tell God, "You're in charge" and then turn around and say, "Wait a minute. I don't like this. You'd better come up with a better plan, or I'm out of here." After years of glibly singing, "I surrender all," I finally did.

That's not to say I haven't questioned why God has not allowed me to sing as I once did. I have. But with time I have come to see the wisdom in His plan. Every time I step out onto a stage and grab a microphone, I am humbly reminded that I am not in charge of the universe. It is only by God's grace that I still have a career in music and that I can sing at all. On those days when I am tempted to relax my standards and thereby reopen the door to the lifestyle that put me on a slippery slope toward Sodom, all I have to do is sing. As the first note comes out of my mouth, I remember the price of my sin. But I consider that a small price to pay for the rich life I now enjoy with God.

The apostle Paul also had some sort of "thorn in his flesh." Three times he pleaded with God to remove it (see 2 Corinthians 12:7-8). God gave him the same answer He gave me: "My grace is sufficient for you, for my power is made perfect in weakness" (12:9, NIV). Paul concluded, "Therefore I will boast all the more gladly about my weaknesses, so that Christ's power may rest on me. That is why, for Christ's sake, I delight in weaknesses, in insults, in hardships, in persecutions, in difficulties. For when I am weak, then I am strong" (12:9-10, NIV). God has now given me the privilege of living these verses.

I've learned to embrace my new singing voice. Today I sing for an audience of One. I must say that considering all I put God through, I am so thankful He still allows me to sing for His glory! What a great blessing.

13

CLEANING HOUSE

The easiest and most effective way to beat sin is to stay away from anything that stirs up temptation. Obviously, no one can get away from every source of temptation, at least not on this side of the grave. And we can't completely escape the power of the flesh. As long as we live on this earth, we will be vulnerable. Someone once asked Clay how long it took before he didn't feel tempted by pornography and lust. He laughed. That day hasn't yet arrived. It probably never will. Every day is a battle against his flesh and the devil. Lust is Clay's area of greatest weakness, his Achilles heel. Because of this, he needs more than willpower to overcome the cycle of porn and lust.

Jesus said, "Anyone who even looks at a woman with lust in his eye has already committed adultery with her in his heart. So if your eye — even if it is your good eye — causes you to lust, gouge it out and throw it away. It is better for you to lose one part of your body than for your whole body to be thrown into hell" (Matthew 5:28-29). Clay could take His words literally and yank his eyes out (both of them have done a pretty good job of looking lustfully at women), but he really didn't want to go through the rest of his life blind. Besides, Jesus didn't mean for us to walk around with empty sockets where eyeballs used to be. Scripture also says, "Run from anything that stimulates youthful lust. Follow anything that makes you want to do right" (2 Timothy 2:22). So instead of plucking out his eyes, Clay got rid of all the material he'd used to get the lust motor revving. But he couldn't do this alone. This needed to be a team effort.

THROWING OUT THE VIDEOS (CLAY)

Driving home from my meeting with Chris Beatty, I knew I had to destroy my pornographic videos. I didn't do this the minute I got home because I hadn't yet decided how I would explain all this to Renee. One afternoon while she was gone, I took the tapes outside and smashed them and then threw the broken pieces of plastic in the garbage can and covered them with more trash. The process only took a few minutes, as my entire collection consisted of two or three tapes. As I said earlier, I didn't need new videos with different plot lines to keep my attention. The images burned themselves into my brain, so I could recreate the pornographic experience anywhere at any time by simply closing my eyes and replaying them in my mind. (We will explore how to overcome this part of pornography's hold in the next chapter.)

Destroying my porn collection solidified my repentance from this sin. There had been times in the past when I'd tried to tell myself that I was through with porn, but as long as the videos stayed in the closet, I knew I would go back. Getting rid of them didn't make a relapse impossible, but it made it much more difficult. Throwing them out was also an act of prayer. "Okay, God," I said as I opened the trash can, "I'm throwing this smut out. Please, oh, please, keep me from ever falling into this trap again."

As I walked back into the house, I let out a sigh of relief. I felt cleaner, as if I'd just had a bath. And I also felt safer. For the first time in a long time, I wouldn't hear the siren song of those tapes calling to me from the back of the closet. As I went through the living room, a smile broke out across my lips. *Man, I'm glad that's done,* I told myself.

But I wasn't finished cleaning house. Once I'd removed porn from the equation, my flesh started looking around for some other source of fuel for the lust machine. It didn't have to look far. The mainstream movies that left little to the imagination were still available every night on our cable channels. The Victoria's Secret catalog still sat on the nightstand next to our bed, and *Glamour* and *Cosmo* were on the coffee table. "This is going to be a lot harder than I thought," I said to myself. "I'm going to need help."

OPEN EYES (RENEE)

Clay never came to me and said, "Renee, we've got to stop renting R-rated movies and we're never going to watch *Sex and the City* again." Instead he simply stopped watching those things. He never made a big deal about it, and he didn't come up with a list of rules about what we would and would not watch. More than once he excused himself from the living room when a show featured bikini-clad models or other images he knew he could not handle. He even turned off *Monday Night Football* when the cameramen seemed overly enamored with the cheerleaders. That's when I started to understand the hold this sin had on him and the lengths he was willing to go to get out of it.

The problem wasn't just the porn but the lust it stirred up. The more I understood Clay's weakness, the more sensitive I became to the sexually charged material that surrounds us. It was as though my eyes were opened to it for the first time. The images are everywhere. Bikinis, tight sweaters, cleavage — everywhere I looked, there they were! Car commercials. Liquor ads in the middle of *Sports Illustrated*. The lingerie ads in the Sunday paper. Even many supposedly family-friendly movies. The people who make these things must think the only way to get noticed is to target the basest instincts in people because that's where they aim.

As Clay and I worked through his problem, I tried to protect him from as much of this material as I could. I turned magazine covers over in airports and steered us down another aisle if I spotted an attractive woman up ahead. I know I went a little overboard in the beginning, but I was desperate. I felt as if I had to do everything I could to keep any and every source of temptation away from Clay.

Then one afternoon I pulled the mail out of the mailbox and started thumbing through it as I walked up the driveway to the house. *Great, a new Victoria's Secret catalog*, I said to myself. I loved ordering things from them. I would even take the catalog over to Clay and point to a model wearing some lingerie I liked and ask him, "Do you think this would look good on me?" But that afternoon it suddenly hit me: *I'm only making things worse!* The images in the catalog left little to the imagination, and showing them to a man struggling to overcome lust was like taking a recovering alcoholic into a bar. Here I was trying to steer my husband away from random women at the local grocery store while I invited scantily clad women into our house through this catalog. Talk about straining out a gnat and swallowing a camel (see Matthew 23:24)!

I walked into the house and motioned toward the catalog. "Clay," I asked, "does this thing bother you?"

"Honestly, yes," he said. "I wish you wouldn't get those catalogs anymore. They're a real struggle for me." I called and canceled them that day.

Of course, I can't protect Clay from every possible source of temptation. However, I don't have to make his struggle any more difficult by bringing things into our home that will stir up lust in him. That's why I don't buy most of the magazines I used to enjoy. Nor do we watch much television or rent many movies anymore.

It's not that every television show is evil or that the Bible is the only thing we can read in our home. Television in and of itself is not bad, nor does a magazine have to be published by Focus on the Family in order to be acceptable. But I have chosen to limit my own freedom in Christ in order to help my husband in his area of weakness. The Bible addresses this issue in 1 Corinthians 8:9-13:

> But you must be careful with this freedom of yours. Do not cause a brother or sister with a weaker conscience to stumble.
>
> You see, this is what can happen: Weak Christians who think it is wrong to eat this food will see you eating in the temple of an idol. You know there's nothing wrong with it, but they will be encouraged to violate their conscience by eating food that has been dedicated to the idol. So because of your superior knowledge, a weak Christian, for whom Christ died, will be destroyed. And you are sinning against Christ when you sin against other Christians by encouraging them to do something they believe is wrong. If what I eat is going to make another Christian sin, I will never eat meat again as long as I live — for I don't want to make another Christian stumble.

If the photographs in *People* make my husband stumble, I will never buy a *People* magazine again. If the lingerie ads in the Sunday paper stir up lust in him, I will remove them before he opens the paper. If having Internet access proves to be too great a temptation for him, ours will become one of the few nonwired houses in America. When God opened my eyes, He made me keenly aware of Clay's areas of temptation. My goal in this is to help my husband flee from temptation.

LEARNING TO DISCERN

Saying we need to sweep the house of anything that might cause Clay to stumble sounds simple enough, but learning where to draw the line can be tough. It would be easy for us to become legalistic with the standards we establish about what we will and will not let into our home and to start looking down on everyone who subscribes to *Sports Illustrated* with its annual swimsuit issue. Or we could become so afraid of evil influences that we never leave the house. In those early days, we bounced around some extreme ideas as we tried to find a balance that worked for us.

Through a process of trial and error, we discovered that rather than laying down rules or trying to hide from the world completely, we needed to make the act of cleaning house an act of faith. The choices we make about the books, magazines, television shows, and movies we expose ourselves to now grow out of a three-way conversation we have among God and ourselves. Above all, we ask how watching a movie such as *Signs* or *Closer* or even *Rugrats* will affect our walk with God. Some of these conversations are very short. When the small print under a movie's rating says, "Contains nudity, sexual content, and graphic violence," it is easy to figure out that watching it will not make us more like Jesus. Because the advertisements and program descriptions don't always tell us what to expect in the middle of a movie, we go to www.screenit.com and check shows out before we buy tickets. This site and others, such as Focus on the Family's www.pluggedinonline.com, give detailed content descriptions that help us make an informed decision as to whether a particular movie is something God would want us to see.

Not all the choices are obvious. For that we need God to speak up in this conversation. Of course, He never yells down from heaven saying something such as, "*Signs* is a good movie. Enjoy it." Nor does His Word have a verse that says, "*Dodgeball* may only be rated PG-13, but it contains sexual references and crude humor that are offensive." But the Bible does tell us, "For though your hearts were once full of darkness, now you are full of light from the Lord, and your behavior should show it!" (Ephesians 5:8). So to put this verse into practice, we learn as much as we can about a particular show and ask ourselves, *How does this show measure up to this passage?*

For example, *Signs* tells the story of an alien attack and the way it changes the lives of a family in rural Pennsylvania. But the real story goes much deeper. The film takes us inside the life of Graham Hess, a former pastor, who rejected God after his wife was killed in a tragic accident. As the movie unfolds, we find Graham locked in a battle with God even as the aliens invade his home. The movie has a happy ending, but even if it didn't, it has a powerful message. It forces us to examine whether God is truly in control of our lives and if we can live with that conviction when our lives take unexpected and unwanted turns. Although the movie contains a few uses of profanity, overall it is a good film with a positive message. However, if the movie took place on a beach in Malibu and the preacher's family was replaced with surgically enhanced, blonde knockouts in tight t-shirts and form-fitting shorts, we wouldn't go see it. The message wouldn't be worth wading through the sexual imagery.

Cleaning out sources of temptation requires more than throwing away a pile of magazines and canceling cable channels. By turning our choices into opportunities to seek God and His wisdom, we draw closer to Him and to one another. The two of us have made a conscious effort to keep this process from turning into something cold and legalistic.

The Bible says that everything that does not come from faith is sin (see Romans 14:23). The context of this verse applies directly to decisions such as those we've discussed in this chapter. Cleaning out sources of temptation does more than protect our family from sin; it forces us to trust God and to listen for His voice. This sets the stage for the next step in this process.

14

WINNING THE BATTLE OF THE MIND

We had to remove from our home everything that caused Clay to stumble. However, pornography by its nature acts like a cancer in the mind. The images seep deep into the inner recesses of the thought life. Then, when you least expect it, they jump back to the forefront, and it's as if you are watching them all over again. You can't just delete pornographic images from your memory or simply decide not to think about them.

Yet the Bible says, "For as [a man] thinks in his heart, so is he" (Proverbs 23:7, NKJV). This means that whatever we allow our minds to dwell on will determine the direction of our lives. Clay's battle against the cycle of lust came down to the battlefield of the mind. We could turn off the television and cancel magazine subscriptions, but what could we do about the pornographic images that had already infiltrated his mind? Finding an answer was crucial to winning this battle.

GOD'S REALLY POWERFUL SOAP (CLAY)

When I came face-to-face with my sin, I felt very dirty. They don't call porn "filth" for nothing. That's how it leaves you feeling. The repeated exposure to it and the constant replaying of those scenes in my mind made me feel as though my brain needed a steam cleaning. Fortunately, God not only understands the power of sin, but He also has a remedy. The day I asked Christ to forgive me, He took away the offense of my sin. In God's eyes, it was as if I had never fantasized about other women or committed any of the other offensive acts I'd made a habit of doing. Jesus' blood made me white as snow as I stood before the Father. But God doesn't stop there.

Even though I had asked God to forgive me, I still had memories of what I'd done and seen. He didn't just pluck them out of my head, nor did He make it impossible for me to revisit them whenever I wanted. Instead, He gave me a promise: "Christ loved the church and gave himself up for her to make her holy, cleansing her by the washing with water through *the word*" (Ephesians 5:25-26, NIV, emphasis added). This verse tells me that Christ wants to make me holy; He wants to clean me up inside and out. Thankfully, it also tells me how He is going to do it: through His Word, the Bible.

I know this sounds pretty simplistic. *Read the Bible and those bad thoughts will go away? Is that what you are telling me, Clay?* Yes and no. Simply running your eyes up and down the pages of the Bible won't set anyone free from years of viewing porn. I know from experience. I knew parts of the Bible from sitting in church all those years, but that hadn't kept me out of porn.

However, after I rededicated my life to Christ, I found that God gave me an insatiable appetite for more of Him. I wanted to know Him better. My appetite for God led me to His Word. I didn't just read a few Bible verses here and there; I devoured it. I started a Bible-reading schedule that would take me through the Bible in a year. Renee soon joined me. I dove into the Bible and quickly realized that what I was reading was the truth, it was perfection, and it was the purest thing I had ever soaked in. No words can adequately describe the experience.

It felt as if I had come into the house after spending three or four hours digging up tree stumps on a hot, humid August afternoon in Memphis and jumped into a cool shower. God's Word not only cleansed my mind; it also refreshed my spirit.

MAKING EVERY THOUGHT OBEDIENT TO CHRIST (CLAY)

This is not to say that my struggles with impure thoughts ended when I started reading the Bible every day. Like I said in the last chapter, I still face this battle each and every day. Those images can still come back to haunt me, and my flesh doesn't help matters. My eyes want to roam around the room, looking for some hot babe to lock on to. It's my own fault. I trained them to do that back when I thought about sex nonstop. But even though I can't block such thoughts from coming into my mind, I don't have to dwell on them. I can choose to meditate on the truth of God's Word, truths I have committed to memory so that I can bring them to the forefront of my mind at any time.

So when my thoughts start to run down a path that says, "Wow, check out that girl over there. She's really . . . " I recite Philippians 4:8 to myself: "Fix your thoughts on what is true and honorable and right. Think about things that are pure and lovely and admirable. Think about things that are excellent and worthy of praise." Then I go back over each part of the verse. I ask myself, *Okay, Clay, what is true? God's Word is true.* And then I quote specific truths from His Word. For instance:

> Submit yourselves, then, to God. Resist the devil, and
> he will flee from you. Come near to God and he will
> come near to you. (James 4:7-8, NIV)

121

Therefore do not let sin reign in your mortal body so
that you obey its evil desires. Do not offer the parts
of your body to sin, as instruments of wickedness,
but rather offer yourselves to God, as those who have
been brought from death to life; and offer the parts
of your body to him as instruments of righteousness.
For sin shall not be your master, because you are not
under law, but under grace. (Romans 6:12-14, NIV)

Then I ask myself, *What is honorable? Being faithful to Renee is
honorable. Obeying God's command not to lust is honorable....* And so
on. I go through each part of the verse like this, and before I know it,
the wrestling match against temptation gives way to singing songs of
praise to God.

Early on, I had a difficult time doing this. I'd made a habit of looking
around for a beautiful woman in public places, especially airports, and
plugging her into the fantasies that I constantly played in my head. The
first time I went to an airport after telling God I was going to get serious
about following Him, I broke out in a cold sweat. I felt like a guy on a
strict diet walking through a chocolate factory. As my eyes started to
search, I began to pray. Pretty soon my prayer became a song — actually
more of a chant. I started reminding myself over and over, *Jesus Christ
is Lord of all. Jesus Christ is Lord of all.* I didn't care if anyone saw my lips
moving or if I had a wide-eyed, deer-in-the-headlights look on my face.
Second Corinthians 10:5 says to take every thought captive and make it
obedient to Christ, and that's what I did. To win the battle of the mind,
we have to take some prisoners and show them no mercy.

A NEW WAY OF THINKING (RENEE)

Clay wasn't the only one who needed to make changes in his thinking. I did too. Romans 12:2 says, "Don't copy the behavior and customs of this world, but let God transform you into a new person by changing the way you think." I'd done the opposite. I had copied the behavior and customs of the world and absorbed its wisdom.

Whenever we traveled, I was a sucker for magazines that had stories with titles such as, "10 Ways to Please Your Man" or "What Every Man Wants His Woman to Know." I would pore over fashion magazines such as *In Style, Cosmopolitan,* and *Glamour* and home and garden magazines such as *House Beautiful* and *Architectural Digest.* I would look through the pictures, read the articles, and take in all the advice about how to keep my husband happy or be successful or create a home that others would envy. Even though 1 Corinthians 3:19 says the wisdom of the world is foolishness in God's sight, that was all the wisdom I took in back in those days. I allowed the world to tell me how to dress, how to work, how to live, how to be a lover to my husband. I let the media, rather than God's Word, shape the way I thought, and as a result, I bore little resemblance to the person God had created me to be. Through television and movies, I had spent a great deal of time with those who see sex outside of marriage as no big deal, who cuss like sailors, and who mock everything God says is sacred. My attitude and language showed it.

Because of the time I was now spending in His Word, God started changing the way I thought. It wasn't long before I realized I couldn't just veg in front of the television as I once had. In the past I had mindlessly watched any show that caught my fancy, but God was starting to show me that I needed to think about what I was watching so I could evaluate whether it was something I should fill my mind with. A show would come on, and the Holy Spirit would whisper, "Can you hear the message behind this show? How do you think it compares to what God wants to see in your life?" I would look down at one of my daughters sitting beside me, and the thought would flash through my head, *Does this program model behavior I want to see in her life?* I never used to give a second thought to the message behind an advertisement, show, or article, but God was helping me realize that I need to think about the underlying meaning rather than just mindlessly soak up everything I read and see.

When Clay and I began reading the Bible together, it was as though scales fell off of my eyes. I felt so ashamed of the life I had been leading and of the things I had considered so important. We had treasured everything that wouldn't last and had blown off that which would. We had moved to Nashville because we thought we absolutely had to be right in the middle of Music City or Clay's career would suffer. We finally realized that the star mentality that permeates Nashville wasn't good for either of us, so we decided to move back to Memphis. Our move was an outward sign of the internal changes God was bringing about in how we thought and how we lived.

Ephesians 5:15 says, "Be very careful, then, how you live — not as unwise but as wise" (NIV). That's ultimately how God wanted us to live our lives. And as we cooperated with Him, He began to cleanse our minds through His Word and enable us to think like He does.

15

WITH A ~~LITTLE~~ [LOT OF] HELP FROM FRIENDS

Everyone who wants to live for the Lord will face opposition. Satan delights in trying to trip us up and in making our lives an embarrassment to the cause of Christ. The Bible calls this spiritual warfare. Ephesians 6:12 says, "For we are not fighting against people made of flesh and blood, but against the evil rulers and authorities of the unseen world, against those mighty powers of darkness who rule this world, and against wicked spirits in the heavenly realms." No one can battle this alone.

Isolation is not good for believers, especially as we try to live in a hostile spiritual environment. God never intended for us to try to go it alone. Ecclesiastes 4:12 says, "A person standing alone can be attacked and defeated, but two can stand back-to-back and conquer. Three are even better, for a triple-braided cord is not easily broken." The two of us worked as a team to get out of the pit of pornography and its aftereffects. But in order to stay out of that pit forever and move on toward the plan God has for our lives, we needed to enlarge our team. We needed a lot of help from our friends.

ACCOUNTABILITY (CLAY)

Even though I went to church and had Christian friends, I had never really allowed my life to become intertwined with theirs. Nor did I want people to ask me tough questions about my walk with Christ. I remember one time early in my career when Wayne Watson took me aside and talked with me about guarding myself against the temptations that come looking for musicians on the road. I appreciated his taking time out for me, and I gave him honest answers, but our paths didn't cross often enough for this to become a regular thing. I had no one in my life to hold me accountable on a consistent basis.

Accountability is an absolute must for those who want to escape the bondage of pornography and never go back. James talks about it when he writes, "Confess your sins to each other and pray for each other so that you may be healed" (5:16). I needed someone in my life I could call and say, "Satan's hit me hard today. I need your prayers."

Shortly after we moved back to Memphis, I went to a Christian friend whose walk I respect and whose integrity I can trust and asked him to hold me accountable in my daily life. I gave him a free hand to ask me anything about my life at any time. I told him that nothing is off-limits. I asked him to grill me about the movies and television shows I watch, the amount of time I spend with Renee and our girls, and how much time I spend alone with God. And I told him that I especially want him to look me in the eye and ask, "Clay, how's the lust factor?" Sure, I can lie to him and tell him everything in my life is exactly as it should be, but what purpose would that serve? I've kept too many secrets for too long. I no longer want to live that way. I want to be a man of complete honesty and integrity. That's why I asked my friend to always end our talks with the question, "Have you lied to me in any of your answers?"

My accountability partner encourages me when this constant fight against the same old temptation starts to get me down. Some days I wish I could let my guard down without having to worry about getting blindsided, but my friend tells me to keep at it, to not give up, and to know that he's praying for me. I know he has my back, just as I have his.

Finding an accountability partner wasn't easy. It had to be someone who didn't see me as Clay Crosse, recording star, but as just an ordinary guy. More important, this person needed to have a strong walk with Christ, the courage to speak the truth in love even when it hurts, and tight lips that will never utter a word of what I might share with him. I'd never made much of an effort to build close relationships with people who fit that description because I was so focused on my career. We had Christian friends, but many of them were just like we were before God got our attention. We didn't hang out with spiritual fireballs who would make us feel convicted every time we told an off-color joke or went to a movie with a lot of steamy scenes. But God knew I was serious about winning this battle against pornography, and when we moved back to Memphis, He led me to the right person.

AN EXTENDED FAMILY (CLAY)

After moving back home to Memphis in 1999 and serving at our home church for a few years, Renee and I both felt a strong calling to join a brand-new church in the area. That church is The Love of Christ Church (TLC for short). TLC has now been our home for the past few years. We serve there, I as worship pastor and Renee on the leadership team for women's activities, alongside Pastor Dana Key (yes, that's the same Dana Key who led the Christian rock group DeGarmo and Key for so many years). Serving as worship pastor at TLC has been an incredible blessing in my life.

As we worked to help get this new church off the ground, I began to understand just how important church is in the life of a believer. Even though I'd gone to church my entire life, I'd never realized how much I needed this group of people I now saw as family. The Bible calls the church "the body of Christ" (1 Corinthians 12:12). Paul wrote that believers need to be connected to a local church just as a hand or foot has to be connected to a human body to survive. *No wonder I've struggled so much,* I told myself. *I've been that disconnected foot trying to stay alive even though I'd chopped myself off from the rest of the body.*

Don't get me wrong. Church had always been important to me. Renee and I loved our home church, and we were members of a great church in Nashville. But it is one thing to go to a church and another thing entirely to allow God to connect our lives to the lives of the people around us. Even though I'd been a church member, I had tried to live the Christian life alone. Through serving at TLC, I learned not to fly solo any longer. Everyone in our church knows the details of our past that Renee and I share in this book, but no one looks at me as though I am some kind of phony for the secret life I used to live, nor do they think I'm a sicko because of what I once did. My past doesn't matter here, the good or the bad. We collectively share the love of Christ with one another. That's the help I need from my friends.

Becoming a local church worship leader marked a dramatic shift in my life. I'd never done anything like this because I was always too wrapped up in myself. But God told me to start serving others. After much prayer, Renee and I felt God telling us that even if it meant I should slow down my career on the road, I should begin to put more focus and energy into this local church. Keep in mind that TLC was a brand-new church. They could not afford to pay me a full salary, but God didn't seem overly concerned about that at the time. I cut back my concert schedule and broke my contract with my record label after the release of my 2000 CD, *A Different Man*. It's funny because in the past I was entirely focused on becoming a star. Now I just want to use the gifts God has given me to lift Him up and serve other people.

I said a moment ago that my past doesn't matter at TLC. That's not entirely correct. The leaders of our church know about my past, and they pray for me so that the past stays in the past. These men are dear friends and are vital in supporting me in my walk with Christ.

BUILDING THE RELATIONSHIP WE ALWAYS WANTED

Clay and Renee

16

DISCOVERING GOD'S DESIGN FOR MARRIAGE

Gaining victory over Clay's battle with pornography and lust was only half of the challenge we faced. His secret life called into question everything we'd ever believed about our relationship. The closeness, the oneness of thought and mind, even the vow to love one another looked shaky in the aftermath. Even months down the road we still felt the fallout of what had happened. We couldn't just go back to life as normal because normal didn't exist anymore. Our marriage had to be rebuilt from the ground up.

Two things made this rebuilding possible. First and foremost was God's grace. God used this worst-case scenario to get our attention and pull us back to Him. As a result, we rededicated our lives to Christ and made a fresh start with God. Our new beginning with the Lord led to a new beginning with each other. His grace made forgiveness between us possible and also kept the load of guilt, anger, and bitterness from crushing us completely. We cannot emphasize this enough: Our marriage not only survived, but we have become even closer because of the spiritual intimacy we now experience.

The second essential for being able to rebuild was the commitment we had to one another. Even with everything that had happened, neither of us considered walking away from the other. This commitment was pushed to its absolute limit, but it survived. If you don't understand how, then you need to reread the last paragraph. As we looked around and surveyed the damage done to our relationship, we both said, "How are we going to fix this?" instead of "I don't think this is going to work." Our commitment enabled us to do the hard work of rebuilding our marriage. Nothing about this was easy. We both shed many tears and had days when we wondered how much we could stand. But we were there. We weren't going anywhere. If either of us had said in the back of our minds, "I'll give this a couple of months, and if things don't change, I'm out of here," it wouldn't have worked. By God's grace and our mutual commitment to our vows, our marriage, our family, and our lives were completely transformed.

But we're jumping ahead of ourselves. Before we could rebuild our home, we needed some kind of plan, some sort of blueprint, to ensure that we did things right. Obviously, what we did before hadn't worked, although at the time we thought it was working. While we were happy with our lives and our relationship, most of our happiness was built on shaky ground: fame, success, money, and material comfort. As the Bible says, we'd built our home on the sand (see Matthew 7:24-27). When the rains came down, our foundation was washed away and our home crashed. After experiencing a fresh start with God and the joy of His forgiveness, we wanted to build our home on the Rock that would never let us down.

BUILDING A STRONG FOUNDATION (RENEE)

Marriage was God's idea. When He created the human race, He initially made only one person, Adam. God placed Adam in the garden He'd made for him and then brought all the animals past him in pairs so that Adam could give them names. Then God said, "It is not good for the man to be alone. I will make a companion who will help him" (Genesis 2:18). By himself, Adam was incomplete. So God put him into a deep sleep, took one of his ribs, and made Eve out of the rib. Then God woke Adam and presented him with his bride. Adam's first words when he saw Eve were, "At last!" (2:23). He wasn't lying when he told her he'd been waiting for her all his life.

Some people say the story of Adam and Eve is nothing more than a myth or legend. But whether we believe the story or not doesn't change the fact that it is literally true. Long ago these events happened exactly as the Bible says. Adam and Eve didn't live in the Garden of Eden by themselves; God was with them. He created them to know Him and love Him, and they lived in perfect relationship with Him. Revelation 21:7 sums up how they experienced God: "And I will be their God, and they will be my children." This is still God's plan. The story of Adam and Eve is important to more than just theologians and preachers because it gives us insight into God's plan for marriage. He designed marriage to be a place where we can know Him and experience Him together.

As you know, before 1998 God wasn't a priority in either of our lives, let alone in our marriage. As we sought to rebuild our marriage, we realized that it needed to be built on the firm foundation of God. He must be the most important thing in our lives and in our marriage. Jesus told us that we have to love Him more than we love anyone else, even the person we've pledged to love, honor, and cherish until death (see Luke 14:26). If we hadn't done this, our marriage never would have survived, let alone thrived.

Over the next few chapters you will read about some of the other changes we made, but none of them had the impact this one had. We firmly believe that if couples will get up every day and make the conscious decision to put Christ first over each other, their marriage will be successful 100 percent of the time. It has worked for us.

AN EVERYDAY DECISION (CLAY)

I can just hear the cynics: "Oh, c'mon, Clay and Renee! Get real. There is absolutely no 100 percent guarantee for a successful marriage. Marriages are too different, too diverse. The challenges and problems of marriage are just too complicated and varied to attempt to pin down success with a guarantee for survival and happiness." While we do agree that marriages face too many challenges to list, we know that giving oneself completely to Christ will make any marriage work well. Period.

If I had given my life completely to Jesus every day and followed Him closely, I never would have made having fun my first priority. If my focus had been on pleasing God, I never would have viewed pornography, nor would I have started entertaining perverse fantasies. Don't misunderstand what I am saying. I am *not* saying that Christian couples will never have any problems or fall into sin. Remember, Renee and I had grown up in church. We'd both asked Jesus to be our Savior. After we were married, we went to church most Sundays. We tithed. We did almost everything a Christian is supposed to do. But our focus was always on ourselves. God was always a means to an end.

To get our lives and marriage back on track, we had to stop playing games with God and instead give everything up to Him. This isn't a one-time decision; it's a decision both of us need to make every day. Even today I struggle to keep Christ first. If I am not careful, I will start obsessing over my career or over the church where I serve as worship pastor or even over something as insignificant as a basketball team. I have to rededicate myself to Christ every single day.

BECOMING THE SPIRITUAL LEADER (CLAY)

It's one thing to say you are going to put God first in your marriage, and it's another thing to do it. As I searched the Bible to try to understand God's plan for our marriage, I came across Ephesians 5:23. This verse says that the husband is the head of his wife, just as Christ is the head of the church. This does not mean I am Renee's boss, the king of the Crosse castle, and that she is my handmaiden to do my bidding. As I read the verse in the context of the rest of Ephesians, I realized God gave me the responsibility of spiritual leadership in my marriage and in my home. For the first eight years of our married life, I'd shirked that responsibility. Long before I failed Renee morally by lusting after other women, I had failed her in this regard. If I were serious about putting Christ first in everything, I had to start doing what He told me to do in my home.

I have to be honest with you. The thought of stepping forward after my confession and telling Renee, "God made me the spiritual leader of this home" intimidated me to death. What kind of spiritual leader was I? Just a few weeks earlier, I'd been orchestrating my own personal porn videos in my head, and now I was supposed to help Renee get closer to God? Yeah, right. And who would want to follow a leader with my track record? But God took away my fears by taking me back to Ephesians 5. There I read:

> Husbands, love your wives, just as Christ loved the church and gave himself up for her to make her holy, cleansing her by the washing with water through the word, and to present her to himself as a radiant church, without stain or wrinkle or any other blemish, but holy and blameless. In this same way, husbands

ought to love their wives as their own bodies. He who loves his wife loves himself." (25-28, NIV)

Through these verses God told me that the best way to lead my home was by loving Renee in the same way Jesus loves her, and that's what I started trying to do. I asked God to love Renee through me. That's when I started praying for her and with her and devouring my Bible and inviting her to join me in that. These may seem like small things, but they were crucial in moving our family away from a self-centered, casual approach to God and toward being serious about following Him. (The next chapter takes a closer look at how God expects husbands to love their wives.)

I'm committed to becoming a godly man of integrity who leads his family by example. Yet I'm struck with a sad thought. If these had been my priorities from the day Renee and I first said, "I do," we could have avoided the pit we fell into. There wouldn't have been an aftermath if I had done the "beforemath."

I can't undo the past, but I can change the future. That is why, in the words of the apostle Paul, "I am focusing all my energies on this one thing: Forgetting the past and looking forward to what lies ahead, I strain to reach the end of the race and receive the prize for which God, through Christ Jesus, is calling us up to heaven" (Philippians 3:13-14).

LETTING HIM LEAD (RENEE)

God called Clay to be the spiritual leader of our home, and He expects me to let my husband lead. Ephesians 5:22-24 says, "You wives will submit to your husbands as you do to the Lord. For a husband is the head of his wife as Christ is the head of his body, the church; he gave his life to be her Savior. As the church submits to Christ, so you wives must submit to your husbands in everything." Believe me, obeying these verses wasn't easy for me, especially in the beginning. Clay didn't exactly have a sterling record. When he told me some of the details of his past fantasies, I was horrified. If I had submitted to his desires for me, my life would have become as sick as his. Because I've seen some wacky interpretations of this passage, I want to clarify what it does not mean.

Scripture makes it clear that God's command to wives to submit to their husbands does not extend to following them into sinful behavior. Remember, Christ comes first. We have to obey Him above all. If submitting to Clay leads me away from Christ, I have to obey God, not my husband. God wants me to commit myself to Him completely. If someday I have to choose between obeying Christ or submitting to my husband, I will choose Christ.

This passage also does not mean that a wife should allow herself to be abused or treated as a doormat. God's plan for the home is that both the husband and the wife will put Him first, not that men will elevate themselves to kings and reduce their wives to doormats. Believe me, this southern girl ain't gonna be a doormat to anyone! In Ephesians 5:21, husbands and wives are *both* told to submit to one another out of reverence to Christ. This doesn't mean a husband unilaterally makes all the decisions and then informs his wife about them and expects her to go along with them. Instead, I think this verse means that God wants me to allow Clay to lead our home without second-guessing everything he does or constantly criticizing him for the decisions he makes. Most of the time before we make any kind of decision, we talk it through and pray about it together. We both want to know God's will, and once we know what His will is, we try to do it. Clay is the leader because he is the one who sets the spiritual climate in our household. He has to answer to God for how well he does this. That's a very heavy responsibility. I know I am now blessed with a husband who wants God's best for me and for my family. Letting a man like that lead is easy.

LOVE WAS NOT ALL WE NEEDED

Every fairy tale ends with the words "and they lived happily ever after." This implies that marriages need only romantic love to succeed. But we found that isn't enough. The giddy feeling of being "in love" doesn't last. We thought it would when we were first married; now we know better. Building a home according to God's blueprint takes a great deal of time and effort. But the end result is worth it.

17

CHOOSING LOVE

Our spiritual problems resulted from a failure to keep the first and greatest commandment. Neither of us loved the Lord with all our heart, soul, mind, and strength. Instead we loved the world and everything in it, all the while clutching a ticket to heaven purchased by Jesus with His blood on the cross. The Bible says we are saved by grace, not works (see Ephesians 2:8-9). This is a good thing. We would have been in trouble had we been trying to buy our way into heaven through our behavior. Thankfully, God loved us far too much to abandon us to the mess we'd made of our lives. But of course, you've already read that part of our story.

In turning to pornography, Clay was violating a whole pile of commandments. But there was one in particular he thought he was keeping even as he was stomping it into the ground: "Husbands, love your wives, just as Christ loved the church and gave himself up for her" (Ephesians 5:25, NIV).

LOVE DEFINED (CLAY)

Even while I was giving lust free reign in my life, I told myself I loved Renee and would never walk away from our marriage. I definitely wasn't one of those guys who think that because they said "I love you" once, they don't ever need to say it again. I told Renee I loved her every day, even when I was on the road. But even though I said I loved her, my actions didn't show it. I now realize that I didn't love Renee during those dark days, not in the way Ephesians 5 tells me I must. I felt an emotional attachment to her, but I did not put love into action. If I had, I wouldn't have done the things I did.

I thought I loved Renee because I felt so "in love" with her. But real love has to be more than a feeling. When God tells me to love Renee, He isn't telling me to get butterflies in my stomach when she walks into the room or to experience any of the other emotions we usually associate with being "in love." After all, we can't command our emotions. My feelings fluctuate depending on a variety of factors, from the kind of day I had at the office to what I had for lunch to the movie I just watched. Biblical love, love that lasts, goes beyond feelings. Real love is a decision to love my wife in the same way Jesus loves me.

If you are like me, you are scratching your head, wondering what you have to do to measure up to God's kind of love. But don't worry. God never leaves us in the dark about what He requires of us. When I discovered the thirteenth chapter of the book of 1 Corinthians, I learned exactly what I had to do to love Renee with the love of Christ:

> Love is patient and kind. Love is not jealous or boastful
> or proud or rude. Love does not demand its own way.
> Love is not irritable, and it keeps no record of when it
> has been wronged. It is never glad about injustice but
> rejoices whenever the truth wins out. Love never gives
> up, never loses faith, is always hopeful, and endures
> through every circumstance. (4-7)

Here's the bottom line of what I learned: Instead of simply telling Renee I love her, I have to *show* her love by doing all the things in these verses. That's easier to write than it is to do. Love means being patient. In chapter 11 I wrote about how I had to choose to be patient with Renee as she worked through her emotional reactions to my confession. That exercise in patience was only the beginning of how I need to love her for the rest of our lives. Some days this is easier than others. I'm just like most other guys. There are times when I tap my watch and tell Renee, "Come on, we've got to go!" That's when I need to remember that Mr. Impatience doesn't exactly communicate love in action.

And love is kind. This is perhaps the greatest understatement in the history of humanity. Do we really need to be told that if we love someone, we must be kind to her? We shouldn't, but we do. Often we are most unkind to those we claim to love the most. For me, kindness means anticipating Renee's needs and meeting them without her having to ask. I try to do little things for her. I show her kindness by emptying the dishwasher, rubbing her shoulders at the end of a hard day without expecting anything in return, or calling her while I'm on the road to tell her I'm thinking about her. These small acts of kindness communicate more than any large gift ever could.

The rest of the list in 1 Corinthians 13 is just as convicting. Love doesn't get jealous. That means it trusts implicitly with nothing held back. Love also keeps me from being a blowhard who talks only about myself. And love does not demand its own way. So much for using the head-of-the-home title as an excuse to set up my own little kingdom where it is "my way or the highway." That's not love. That's just rude, and love is not rude.

The biblical definition of love isn't some pie-in-the-sky ideal, completely disconnected to the real world. If it were, the next statement wouldn't be there: Love "keeps no record of when it has been wronged" (1 Corinthians 13:5). I have to say I have benefited from that line more than any man should. Renee never throws my past at me in the middle of an argument (and yes, we still have arguments occasionally, just like any married couple), nor does she hold the things I once did against me. She could, but she doesn't because she loves me. Love keeps no record of when it has been wronged.

Christlike love also lasts forever. This isn't referring to the feelings of love but to the decision to love. When I tell Renee I love her, I am telling her that my love for her will never give up, that I will never toss in the towel and say I can't take this anymore. Every time I say, "I love you," I am telling her that I will always protect her, always trust her, and always love her (see 1 Corinthians 13:7). That's what it means to love my wife as Christ loves the church.

A FULL-TIME PURSUIT (CLAY)

To Renee, the best way I can spell true love is T-I-M-E. Lots and lots of it. I can't squeeze patience and kindness and everything else love requires in between ball games and business trips and lowering my golf handicap. If that means missing a World Series game or doing fewer concerts every year, so be it. I'm not making any kind of sacrifice. I'm simply showing my wife I love her.

In the Old Testament, Jacob fell in love with a girl named Rachel. The only way her father would let Jacob marry her was if Jacob spent seven years working for him without pay. Most guys would have walked away. Not Jacob. He thought the deal was a bargain. The Bible goes on to say, "So Jacob served seven years to get Rachel, but they seemed like only a few days to him because of his love for her" (Genesis 29:20, NIV). That's what true love looks like, and that's what I want to show my wife. I want my actions to say to her, "No one and nothing in the whole wide world means as much to me as you do."

Sadly, this is where many husbands drop the ball. I know a man whose marriage is about to end. He has been unfaithful to his wife without ever looking at another woman. His mistress is college sports. He never misses a game, either by catching it on television or by attending the home games of his favorite team. Although he bought two season tickets, his wife doesn't want to spend all of her free time in the local arena. She feels neglected, as well she should. This man has made it very clear who his first love really is. His words may say, "Baby, I love you," but his actions say something else.

There's no way I could love Renee like this on my own. As my past shows, self-centeredness is my default setting. Left to myself, that's what I will always go back to. But God's grace and the power of the Holy Spirit enable me to do things I would otherwise be unable to do. Every day I pray and ask God to love Renee through me. I can't show her perfect patience or kindness or anything else 1 Corinthians 13 talks about. But God can. Philippians 2:13 makes this promise: "For God is working in you, giving you the desire to obey him and the power to do what pleases him." I remind God of this promise constantly. I can't love the way He wants me to, but He can, and He will through me.

LOVERS AS FRIENDS (RENEE)

While we were dating, Clay and I connected as friends. Whether over the phone or sitting in a booth at Wendy's eating Frosties, we talked about anything and everything. Our friendship grew slowly, and in time we became best friends. We laughed together, we cried together, and we played together. We got to know one another so well that we knew we needed to spend the rest of our lives together.

But our preoccupation with success, fame, and fortune and our self-absorption caused us to slowly drift apart. When Clay's sexual fantasies started spinning out of control, his lust and guilt pulled him even further away from me. If I hadn't been so into myself, I would have noticed the distance that had come between us, but I didn't. It took our crisis to wake us up to the trouble we were in.

After we nearly lost each other, Clay and I rediscovered the joy of just spending time together. We watch much less television than we once did, mainly because we are too busy talking or playing games with our daughters. At one time we were so busy looking for a way to be entertained that we lost sight of one another. We still enjoy watching movies together but not at the expense of communication. We also take walks together, and yes, we even go back to Wendy's for the occasional Frosty, just like we did when we were dating. Choosing to love one another means choosing to remain friends through the years. For us, renewing our friendship is where the healing began.

GOING DEEPER (RENEE)

Clay and I no longer connect simply as best friends. Our relationship is much better than anything we ever had in our six years of dating or our first eight years of marriage. While neither of us was unhappy in our marriage, we had settled for far less than a marriage can be. Today we are closer and more in love than I ever thought possible.

I'm not just saying this to give our story a happy ending. We've been through a lot of self-inflicted pain and shed rivers of tears. Yet along the way, God did something amazing. He changed two self-absorbed, materialistic individuals into real lovers who care far more about the other than they do about themselves. This is true intimacy. It didn't happen overnight, nor did it take place without a lot of work. Since putting God first in our lives, we've been doing some basic things that allow us to touch one another spirit to spirit.

You've already read about how we started praying together. I don't want you to get the wrong impression. The time we spend in prayer isn't some Norman Rockwell painting of the perfect Christian couple. I have to admit, opening up in front of Clay in this way was one of the hardest things I've ever done. The thought of praying in front of my husband just two hours after he'd seen me slamming pots and pans and yelling at them because I couldn't find the one I needed scared me to death. How could I take his hand and sound all pious and Christian after acting anything but? The first few times I prayed in front of Clay I felt awkward and just a little bit silly. I thought the words of my prayer sounded stupid, and once or twice I stumbled over a word. *Great, I thought to myself, he's going to think I don't even know how to pray.*

But a funny thing happened in the middle of my stuttering and stammering. About halfway through the prayer, the Holy Spirit took over. Pretty soon the two of us were pouring our guts out to God. We were both hurting so badly that I guess we forgot about how we sounded. Sometimes neither of us could even get the words out. We just lay on the floor, gripping one another's hands, and crying before God. Even though I didn't want to pray with Clay, I felt my spirit open up, and the emotions flowed out. Both of us could feel the presence of God in the room, touching us, pulling us closer to Him and to each another.

I'd always thought Clay and I were close. But I never experienced anything that approached the closeness God established between us when we broke down and became completely transparent before Him. We are one another's ultimate accountability partners. God uses each of us to help the other when we are most vulnerable. On our knees before Him, we drop our guard and get rid of any masks.

Some people have asked how we survived the mess porn created. This is how: We prayed one another through it. But we didn't just pray together; we ministered to one another. I never knew that could happen.

I would say something like, "I can't pray right now. I'm having a dark day," and Clay would reach over, take my hand, and start praying for me. Talk about intimacy! I'd never experienced anything like that before. When we started opening up our lives spiritually before God and one another, we found a deeper level of intimacy that had nothing to do with sex. When we became transparent before God, we also became transparent to one another. We told each other our deepest feelings and thoughts. We knew where the other was hurting or struggling and where he or she had seen God at work that day.

As a result, we have also become one another's greatest encouragers. We've picked each other up so many times. There were days when Clay was so overwhelmed by guilt that he felt as if he would always be a fraud no matter what he did in the future. "I don't know how God can forgive what I've done. And honestly, Renee, I don't know how you can either," he would say to me. I could have said something like, "You've got that right, buddy," but instead I chose to love him. I would reassure him that I had indeed forgiven him, and then I would read 1 John 1:9 to him. It says, "If we confess our sins to him, he is faithful and just to forgive us and to cleanse us from every wrong." Then we would just hold each other and cry.

To me, that's what it means to choose to love one another. It moves us beyond our past failures and draws us closer than we ever imagined possible. I thought we loved one another before. Now God has given me the privilege of learning what love can really be.

18

RECOVERING PASSION

One of the questions I get asked when we share our story is "How could you give yourself completely to Clay after he violated your wedding vows like he did?" Even though Clay did not commit physical adultery, he committed adultery in his heart when his lust boiled out of control. This lust spilled over into our sex life, tainting the wonderful gift God gave us as a married couple.

Many women say they might be able to forgive their husbands for viewing pornography and lusting after other women, but they couldn't imagine having much of a sex life after such a confession. Thankfully, that hasn't been the case for us. Our sex life is now better than it ever was. But this didn't happen automatically. Just as it took a lot of work for us to rebuild trust and learn to love each other as Christ loves the church, it has taken effort — and God's grace — for us to recover passion.

MY GOAL (RENEE)

Believe me, giving myself physically to Clay wasn't easy when all I could think of was how he had fantasized about other women. But as I said earlier, I always knew that withholding sex from him when he was already struggling with lust would prove counterproductive. How could it help the situation to tell him, "Not tonight, buddy, or for a very, very long time"? With Clay on the road 150 to 200 nights a year, I wanted us to be together when he came home.

But I didn't want that to be the reason for our physical intimacy. I didn't want duty to drive my passion, nor did I just want to get to the point where Clay could touch me without my mind flashing back to the fantasies he'd told me about. I wanted to recover the passion we had when we were first married. And I wanted that passion to be real. I wanted us to give ourselves completely to the other with nothing held back rather than selfishly taking from one another. I longed to bring the purity and holiness that this sin had spoiled back to our bed (see Hebrews 13:4), the kind Genesis 2:25 alludes to when it says, "The man and his wife were both naked, and they felt no shame" (NIV).

Two things made this possible, and I hope it won't sound like a broken record when I tell you what they are. We've already talked about them in earlier chapters. They are repentance and forgiveness. I bet you never thought two things usually associated with altar calls and getting right with God could lead to a great sex life. But they can. In fact, after this type of sin invades a marriage, true physical intimacy cannot occur without them.

REPENTANCE — EYES FOR ONLY ONE (CLAY)

Repentance means a change of mind that results in a change of direction. Through it we acknowledge that our actions have harmed another, and we seek the other's forgiveness. When I repented of the sins I sank into through my use of pornography, I didn't just have to acknowledge that my thoughts and actions were an affront to God; they were also an affront to Renee.

When I obey God and love Renee as Jesus loves me, I not only choose to be patient and kind, but I also choose to see her as *the* most beautiful woman in the entire world. Body and soul, she becomes paradise to me. From head to toe, she is beautiful. No other woman can compare. Why would I even look at anyone else? Her beauty doesn't come from her external appearance, although I find that absolutely gorgeous as well. The Bible says that externals don't last. Proverbs 31:30 puts it this way: "Charm is deceptive, and beauty does not last; but a woman who fears the LORD will be greatly praised." As Renee and I walk with Christ together, her true beauty shines more and more. I can honestly say that on both the inside and outside, Renee has never been more ravishing in my eyes than she is today.

I don't keep this a secret from Renee. She knows she is the only woman on this planet I want to gaze upon. This sounds sort of sappy, but I don't care. Every day I choose to love her and her alone, which also means I choose to see her as the most beautiful woman on this earth. Ultimately, this decision is the greatest cure to a wandering eye and a mind that used to wonder, *What if?* It also gives Renee the freedom to open up to me and make herself vulnerable to me physically.

Seeing Renee as the most beautiful woman on earth also means I notice every part of her. Ephesians 5:28 tells me to love my wife as I love my own body. When it comes to my body, I'm aware of most everything that goes on, including every ache and pain and every irregularity. That's how I'm supposed to love Renee. I try to become hyperaware of everything going on in her life and not just when I'm in the mood for love. I try to listen to her and pay attention to everything she goes through in a day and then act accordingly. Nothing says "I love you" quite like leaving a note under her pillow when she most needs one or drawing a hot bath for her after a hard day.

FORGIVENESS AND PASSION (RENEE)

Once Clay repented of his sin, I needed to offer him forgiveness. Both were key to recovering sexual passion in our marriage. Forgiveness tears down the walls sin builds up and can lead to a new level of intimacy. Luke tells the story of an immoral woman who fell at Jesus' feet, washing them with her tears and anointing them with expensive perfume. One of the Pharisees saw this and couldn't believe Jesus would let this woman get close to him. Jesus read the man's thoughts and told him, "I tell you, her sins — and they are many — have been forgiven, so she has shown me much love. But a person who is forgiven little shows only little love" (7:47). The act of forgiveness can build a bond like no other between the person asking for forgiveness and the one offering it. It's true of our relationship with God and with one another as husband and wife.

I already wrote about how Clay had become distant from me because of his sin and the guilt it caused. And my immediate response when he confessed was to pull away from him and never let him get close to me again. But his honesty and brokenness bridged the gap his sin had created, and when I forgave him, my spirit opened back up to him and his to me. This was true for us first emotionally and then physically. Once the two of us became vulnerable with each other and forgiveness flowed, we were soon in one another's arms.

BIBLICAL PASSION (CLAY)

Renee knows I will pursue her, no matter what the cost or the effort, not to satisfy myself but to give myself to her fully. This leads to the kind of steamy passion God desires married couples to share.

If what I just said surprises you, it shouldn't. God invented sexual passion as well as marriage. He says, "Rejoice in the wife of your youth. . . . Let her breasts satisfy you always. May you always be captivated by her love" (Proverbs 5:18-19). That's pretty steamy for a Bible verse, but it's nothing compared to the Song of Solomon, a book devoted not only to love but also to romance. It might surprise some people to find romance in the Bible, but it shouldn't. After all, God created it, and He wants to see it in marriages.

Listen to a few romantic lines from the Song of Solomon:

> Kiss me — full on the mouth!
>> Yes! For your love is better than wine. . . .
> The sweet, fragrant curves of your body,
>> the soft, spiced contours of your flesh
> Invite me, and I come. I stay
>> until dawn breathes its light and night slips away.
> You're beautiful from head to toe, my dear love,
>> beautiful beyond compare, absolutely flawless.
>> > > (1:2; 4:6-7, MSG)

> The kisses of your lips are honey, my love,
>> every syllable you speak a delicacy to savor.
> Your clothes smell like the wild outdoors,
>> the ozone scent of high mountains.
> Dear lover and friend, you're a secret garden,
>> a private and pure fountain.
> Body and soul, you are paradise,
>> a whole orchard of succulent fruits.
>> > > (4:11-13, MSG)

My lover wouldn't take no for an answer,
and the longer he knocked, the more excited
I became.

(5:4, MSG)

Real romance for me is pretty simple. It starts with having eyes only for Renee, communicating that to her, and then actively pursuing her rather than taking her for granted.

BETTER THAN BEFORE (RENEE)

I shared earlier that I've always battled insecurity. Even before the porn, I wondered what Clay was thinking. I would ask myself, *Am I truly the most important person in his life? Am I the only one he desires?* After he broke on to the Christian music scene, my fears grew even stronger. We found ourselves in the middle of beautiful people with money, power, and influence. Everywhere I looked pretty women fawned over Clay. My old insecurities nearly crushed me. The only way I knew to fight back was in the bedroom. I was determined to have a great sex life with Clay so that he would never feel the need to wander. You already know how well that strategy worked.

However, as God changed our lives, He also transformed our times of intimacy, and we began to experience true oneness. God took away my fears, and we both began to give ourselves to one another as we never had before. Clay stopped looking at sex as a way to get his needs met, and I stopped looking at sex as a way to keep him from straying. Both of us started concentrating on meeting one another's needs rather than satisfying our own desires. For the first time, we were free to completely enjoy each other. Clay began to tell me things about my body that pleased him, though not in a crude or vulgar way as he had sometimes done when he was viewing pornography. Now he sounds more like Solomon in the Song of Solomon. He praises different parts of my body and tells me I am the most beautiful woman in the world and the only woman for him. That may sound corny, but I think all women want to hear these kinds of things from their husbands. And I have to say, the attraction we both feel for one another now is greater than anything we ever experienced before.

I used to think I had to be this wildly aggressive woman to satisfy Clay. Now the two of us simply concentrate on spending time together. We always try to go to bed at the same time, just to have time to talk and to feel one another's touch. Some nights I know it is hard for him to listen to me rant about something that got under my skin that day, but he really tries to pay attention, and this makes me even more attracted to him. Clay knows I need lots and lots of touch, so throughout the day he comes up to me and hugs me or takes my hand. We also focus on actually kissing each other rather than just giving little pecks on the cheek on the way out the door. I love to lock lips with Clay and know that he is so into me.

I no longer worry about someone else catching my husband's eye, but it has nothing to do with what goes on in our bedroom. As both of us give ourselves completely to the Lord, we are now free to give ourselves completely to each other without fear and without reservation. I would never have believed God could so completely transform our marriage in this way. I wonder now why we ever settled for less.

19

SERVING OTHERS

In 1999 Clay started touring with the group Newsong. Their approach to concerts is a little different from what he had always done. He used to think people came to see the show, not to listen to some guy talk on and on. But Russ Lee and Michael O'Brien of Newsong aren't the least bit shy about talking. They share their testimonies and give an altar call every night. And each night people come forward because they want God to change their lives. Some come to give their lives to Jesus, some to straighten out the mess they've made of their lives. Others come because they need special prayer for a problem they face.

Newsong also asks people who want special prayer to turn in prayer request cards during the concert. After the concerts they read through the requests and pray for people by name. As Clay read through their prayer requests, he realized that people were coming to concerts carrying some heavy burdens. Abuse. Addictions. Depression. Fear. Suicidal thoughts. The Holy Spirit kept nudging him, telling him he needed to do more than pray.

FROM WASTED YEARS TO CHANGING LIVES (CLAY)

When I went back on the road alone, I decided to give altar calls after each concert. However, I knew I needed to do more than tell people before the last song, "If you want to get right with God, come on up." I needed to share at least a little of what God has done in my life and then invite people to let God work in their lives as well. Otherwise my invitation would seem way too abrupt. This was a hard step for me. I have delusions of being some great preacher with a special message from God, but really I'm just a guy whose life was changed by God and who wants to invite other people to have this same wonderful experience.

The first night that I told my story, I was more than a little nervous. I didn't know exactly what I was going to say. When the time came, I swallowed hard and just started talking. I said, "Not long ago I had to go to my wife and confess to her that I'd been watching pornographic videos and fantasizing about having sex with other women." If the crowd wasn't listening before, they were then.

Somewhere in my brain a voice screamed, *Stop! You are committing career suicide! Do you know what happens to Christian singers who admit to sexual sin?* But I didn't stop. For the next fifteen minutes I told how I'd made a mess of my life and how God had intervened and turned everything around. Then I asked that those who needed to set things right with God move toward the front. And people came. God actually used what I had to say to touch and change the lives of others.

From that night forward I continued telling my story as a part of my concerts. People always came up afterward to ask me how Renee dealt with all of this. I tried to answer their questions, but I could tell they needed to hear from her directly, so I invited her to join me on stage to give the rest of our story. Now the two of us have a vital ministry together. Would we prefer people not know how we used to be? Are you kidding? I don't enjoy putting my worst days on display for the entire world to see, and neither does Renee. But by allowing God to use our story to touch other people's lives, He is helping us redeem those wasted years.

PARTNERS IN MINISTRY (RENEE)

When Clay first asked me to tell my part of our story, I didn't want to do it. I told him flat out, "No way." I'd never even taught a children's Sunday school class, much less stood up in front of a large crowd of strangers and told them all about the most painful experience of my life. I didn't want any part of that. But then Clay said the most infuriating thing I'd ever heard: "Would you at least pray about this?" What could I say? I finally gave in because I knew Clay wasn't the only one coaxing me up on stage.

I shared my part of the story for the first time in Colorado Springs during a chapel service for the staff of Focus on the Family. As if that wasn't hard enough, Dr. James Dobson was sitting in the front row. I could tell Clay was nervous, even though the stage is his second home. I was petrified. *What have I gotten myself into?* I wondered. I didn't have butterflies in my stomach; I had vultures. But then I stepped up on stage, and God took over. The words started and did not stop until the story was out. Afterward, Dr. Dobson told us we had to take this message everywhere we could. At that moment Clay's career ceased to be his alone. God gave the two of us a ministry.

When Clay first confessed to me, I never in a million years thought I would one day openly share what happened with people all over the country. I wanted to hide, not tell the world the details. Only God could take something so horrible and turn it into our life's message, our ministry. As I came to grips with this calling, I realized it was a sign that God was completing the healing process in our marriage. Our problems had stemmed from the deadly combination of casual Christianity and self-centeredness. If we were going to minister to others, our lives could not be about ourselves any longer. God made it clear that He wanted us to focus on putting ourselves at His disposal, no matter what that might mean.

As we've shared our story with others, it has helped us put our problems in proper perspective. Clay started sharing this story just a few months after God made the changes in our lives, and I wasn't completely over everything yet. That was part of the reason I was so hesitant to go up on stage. I thought I needed more time to put all this behind me. How could I stand up and talk as if I had everything together when I still had dark days when I couldn't get past my anger?

But God made it impossible for me not to share, and now I see the wisdom behind His actions. As long as I focused on trying to get past the problems of the past and fixing my own emotional life, my eyes stayed fixed on me. My needs. My hurts. My struggles. When God told me to tell our story, He also told me it was time for me to stop thinking about myself. Talking on stage led to talking personally with women who found themselves in a similar situation. It didn't take me long to realize that many, many women had it far worse than I did. Before long I'd stopped praying for my own healing and instead started praying for the women who had poured out their hearts to me.

FROM THE STAGE TO THE HOME

RENEE:

Over time it's become easier to tell our story on stage. Almost without fail, women in the audience tell me how much they appreciate my taking time out for them. I have to be honest: Serving such an appreciative audience doesn't take a lot of dying to self. In fact, the thanks and praise can almost become intoxicating. Then I go home, and God slams me with reality.

It's easy to serve people who tell you they appreciate you and only require a little of your time. But it's much harder to serve those you live with every day. The things we do for one another inside the home often go unnoticed. No one looks me in the eye, takes me by the hand, and says, "Thank you so much for taking time out of your busy schedule to wash that load of dirty underwear." God continually has to remind me that He wants me to be a servant who puts others before myself. I remember one time in particular when I went from hearing the applause of hundreds to scooping up cat poop in the span of just a couple of hours. In that moment God basically told me, "Renee, I want you to be a servant all the time, not just when people shower you with praise."

CLAY:

Renee wasn't the only one who heard God's call to be a servant both in our ministry and at home. In fact, the shift from *my* career to *our* ministry made some changes I didn't immediately expect. Sometimes I'm the one who stays home because Renee is on the road to speak at a women's conference or marriage retreat. This role reversal caused me to see Renee in a new light. I try to be her number one prayer warrior. When she goes up on stage, with or without me, I want to pray for her as I have never prayed before. I want God to shine through her and change lives through her words. That's quite a change for a guy who used to love the limelight. Now I find incredible joy in staying in the background and supporting Renee as God uses her.

I've also discovered the joy and closeness that come into a marriage when I serve my wife rather than demand that she serve me. I try to do little things to help her, things that may seem trivial but mean a lot to her. For example, I sometimes fill her car up with gas without her asking me to and without announcing it. In fact, I really love it when she doesn't even notice, as though the car just filled itself up. Or I might call while I'm out running errands just to see if she needs anything. I want to constantly encourage her and build her up as a wife, a mother, and a servant of God. My goal is to make her more like Christ and to meet every one of her needs that I can.

Since Renee and I have adopted the attitude of a servant, the change within our home has been tremendous. I'm not saying there aren't days when one or both of us act selfish and self-centered. We are still human, after all. But we both find far more joy in giving our lives away than we ever did when we demanded our own way. Even though we've listed serving others as the last step in the process of rebuilding our relationship, it was a vital part of strengthening our marriage and building a holy home. Becoming a Christian means making Jesus first in your life, and having a successful marriage requires putting your spouse before yourself. Once God finally pounded these truths through this thick skull of mine, my life changed. I would never go back.

20

OUT OF THE ASHES

When we look back at everything God brought us through, one verse says it all:

> As far as I am concerned, God turned into good what you meant for evil. He brought me to the high position I have today so I could save the lives of many people. (Genesis 50:20)

This is our verse. Even though the evil in our lives came from our own sinful choices, God turned it into something good. He took what should have destroyed us and turned it into something that not only has changed our lives but is changing other lives as well.

But in order to bring about this incredible transformation, God first had to allow us to go to the brink.

HE LET US GO TO THE BRINK

We don't want to suggest that God caused Clay to start viewing pornography. He didn't. James 1:13 says, "God is never tempted to do wrong, and he never tempts anyone else either." However, once we both made a series of bad choices, God let us go where those choices took us. He let us go to the brink of disaster. He wasn't being cruel. Far from it.

We see this as part of the good God brought about from the evil in our lives. He did what He said He would do in Romans 1:24: "So God said [to those who worshipped idols instead of Him], in effect, 'If that's what you want, that's what you get'" (MSG).

The first time the Bible records God doing this is in the book of Numbers when the children of Israel started grumbling about the food God had given them in the wilderness while they were traveling from Egypt to the Promised Land. The Israelites wanted meat, and they were mad at God because He gave them only manna. So God sent a huge flock of quail for them to eat. All they had to do was walk outside and the quail crashed at their feet. No one gathered less than fifty bushels of quail. That's a lot of meat to eat. In fact, they ate so much that they got sick from it.

God did something similar with us. We loved everything this world has to offer, even though 1 John 2:15 says, "Do not love the world or anything in the world. If anyone loves the world, the love of the Father is not in him" (NIV). We grew up hearing this verse, and even though at some level we thought we were obeying it, we weren't. Success, fame, comfort, and fun—that's what our lives were all about. God gave us everything in the world we wanted until it almost destroyed our marriage and Clay's career.

Why do we call this "good"? We're both slow learners, but once we learn a lesson, we learn it. And our experience taught us that giving into our selfish desires and living for ourselves will cost us everything in the end. God used it to show us that the whole direction of our lives and our marriage needed to change—quickly.

Don't for a moment assume that Clay and Renee Crosse are special. The Bible says, "For whoever wants to save his life will lose it, but whoever loses his life for me will save it" (Luke 9:24, NIV). We had to lose the life we had been living in order to live the life of our dreams.

If we hadn't gone to the brink of complete disaster, we likely would have continued our casual approach to God for the rest of our lives and missed out on His greatest blessing, the gift of Himself. This was the second "good" He brought out of the evil in our lives.

OUT OF OURSELVES AND INTO GOD

During the first eight years of our marriage, neither of us ever read more than a few verses of the Bible at a time. Nor did we have much of a prayer life. We prayed during emergencies, the old "Help, God, I'm drowning!" kind of prayers, but that was about it. We never prayed together. Ever. The concept of setting apart time during the day to simply seek God's face was entirely foreign to us. Life was pretty much about us. We thought God was important to us, but in looking back, we now see that we simply wanted Him to be a combination of a grandfather, Santa Claus, and a Doberman pinscher. We wanted Him to love us without asking for anything in return, shower us with blessing, and keep bad stuff away from us.

We might have stayed in spiritual bankruptcy for the rest of our lives, blissfully unaware that we could have anything better. But God used our spiritual and marital crisis to yank our focus off ourselves and place it squarely on Him. He opened our eyes and showed us where our self-centered approach to life was taking us. More than anything, He allowed us to feel the absolute emptiness of our souls. When we thought we had lost everything, we found that the only thing we wanted was God Himself. He replaced our longing for the things of the world with passion for His Son. We have experienced the wonder and glory of His forgiveness. We've felt His arms wrap around us, and we've heard Him whisper His love to us, even though we don't deserve it. The psalmist said, "Taste and see that the LORD is good" (Psalm 34:8). We have. Nothing we experienced in the world can compare.

Every time we share our story at a conference or a concert, we are reminded once again of how much God has done for us. This story might just as easily have had a different ending, but God intervened. He didn't give us what we deserved but instead poured out His grace, the very thing we did not deserve, because He loves us. Why He loves us so much is an absolute mystery. How could anyone ever get used to something so wonderful?

God didn't just save us from a worst-case scenario. Another significant "good" God accomplished was transforming our open-minded, self-centered, and self-indulgent home into a holy one.

FROM OPEN MINDS TO A HOLY HOME

As we said earlier, we once thought grace gave us a license to do anything we wanted with minimal consequences. We thought of ourselves as open-minded, but really we were just using the wonder of God's forgiveness as an excuse for indulging our flesh with anything it wanted. The damage inflicted spread beyond our spiritual lives.

As you know, when we rededicated our lives to the Lord and put Him first, God changed our marriage. Transparent honesty took over. It's not just that we tell each other everything. We now know one another in a way we never did before. Neither of us has any kind of illusions about the other. We know each other inside and out. Every strength, every weakness, every place of vulnerability sits out in the open for both of us to see.

God not only changed our marriage, but He also changed our home. He made sure our daughters grew up in a different home than they otherwise would have. They were both so young when all of this happened that they didn't notice a change, but we did. We used to take them to Sunday school and tell them some of the Bible stories we grew up with, but now we want to do so much more than that. We want to instill in them a passion for God. We want them to truly know Jesus, to have His character reproduced in their lives. The two of us wasted so many years thinking the initial step of asking Christ to save us was all God wanted of us. We're doing everything we can to make sure our girls never reach that conclusion. We want to show them how to love Him with all their heart, soul, mind, and strength.

It takes more than family devotions to instill a passion for the Lord, but they are a good place to start. When we pray with our daughters, we try to have the same kind of honesty we have when it is just the two of us. Every week we memorize a Bible verse together as a family. Throughout the day we work to bring the conversation around to God and what He is doing in our lives. We want our daughters to see God's hand on them and to put Him first in their lives. Instead of just going to church, we involve the entire family in ministry. Our girls help with even the smallest things, such as setting up chairs for the Sunday morning worship services (our church meets in a rented ballroom) and wrapping and distributing gifts to homeless families at Christmas. We want them to experience the joy of keeping Christ first in their lives.

The fourth "good" that God brought from the evil in our lives was taking those wasted years and turning them into a message He wanted both of us to share.

WASTED YEARS TURNED INTO FRUITFUL MINISTRY

For the longest time, we thought of the years we spent chasing after everything the world has to offer as a complete waste. We now understand that when God turns evil into good, He redeems all of it.

When Clay used to sing, he did so as an entertainer. He put on a good show that audiences enjoyed. But God showed us that He wants us to tell the story of what He has done in our lives and home so that others might be drawn to Him and He might be given glory. Clay still sings but for a completely different reason. He used to want audiences to walk away thinking, *Wow, that Clay sure can sing.* Now he wants them to be moved to worship God and serve Him with their lives. All of his concerts end with an invitation for people to respond to God. One or both of us share the story we've written here. The wasted years now touch the lives of others.

Together we speak to couples facing the same sort of crisis we went through and help them find God's grace in the midst of it. Yet even after couples come out of the darkness, they still face the huge task of rebuilding their relationship the right way. We both feel a tremendous burden to help them. Out of the ashes of our own personal tragedy God has raised up what we now call Holy Homes Ministries, which challenges Christians to set themselves apart from Satan's influences that poison so many homes today. Specifically, our ministry focuses on the choices people make regarding television, movies, the Internet, and music that if left unchecked can lead to their desensitization and eventually the destruction of their homes. Ultimately, our goal is to help people build holy, God-honoring marriages and families. We currently offer counseling to families in crisis and reach out to people through seminars and conferences.

That's also why we wrote this book. Our prayer is that God can give others hope and help through our story. This is our challenge to you. The only way out of the mess we make of our lives is by shifting our focus off of ourselves and living for Christ alone. Whether your problem is pornography and lust or something else, the solution is always the same. Today, turn your life, your marriage, your career, your children, your leisure time, your church activity, EVERYTHING! over to God. He is the only real solution and the only answer for your life. If you turn to Him, you will discover that the words of King David's prayer in Psalm 22:5 are as true today as when they were first written:

You heard their cries for help and saved them.
They put their trust in you and were never
disappointed.

NOTES

1. "I Surrender All," copyright 1992 First Verse Music (ASCAP), McSpadden/Smith Music (SESAC).
2. Rick Warren, *The Purpose Driven Life: What on Earth Am I Here For?* (Grand Rapids, MI: Zondervan, 2002), 17.

ABOUT THE AUTHORS

Clay and Renee Crosse live in Memphis, Tennessee. Clay serves as worship pastor at The Love of Christ Church in Memphis (www. tlcmemphis.com), and Renee is in leadership with women's ministries there. They have been married since 1990 and have two daughters, Shelby and Savannah. The Crosse family is also very excited to be adopting a baby daughter from China.

Clay has been the recipient of three Dove Awards, including the 1995 New Artist of the Year, and has had nine number one songs. Some of his most well known are "I Surrender All," "I Will Follow Christ," and "He Walked a Mile."

In addition to serving at his church, Clay performs concerts nationwide, and he and Renee speak at various marriage enrichment conferences.

Clay and Renee are honored to tell their story of God's restoration through this, their debut book.

Mark Tabb is the author of eight books, including *Greater Than: Thoughts on the Infinite God* and the 2004 Gold Medallion finalist, *Out of the Whirlwind.* His work has appeared in *Discipleship Journal, Rev, Leadership, HomeLife*, the *Kansas City Star*, and many other publications. Mark is also a contributing editor for Purpose Driven Ministries. In addition to his work as a writer, Mark serves as a volunteer firefighter and chaplain for his local fire department. He and his family live in Indiana.